READING

Taking the critique of writing in the *Phaedrus* as a starting point –
where Socrates argues that a book cannot choose its reader nor can it
defend itself against misinterpretation – *Reading Plato* offers solutions to the problems of interpreting the Platonic dialogues.

- What was Plato's intention in writing dialogues, not treatises?
- Did he choose the dialogue-form in order to hide his own views
  and so preserve what modern interpreters have called 'Platonic
  anonymity'?
- What did he mean by his severe criticism of writing?
- Did he have an oral philosophy, as reported by Aristotle?

Thomas A. Szlezák persuasively and eruditely argues that the dialogues are designed to stimulate philosophical inquiry by turning
readers' souls, as far as writing can achieve this, to the love of wisdom
(*philo-sophia*). The dialogues introduce them to the art of arguing
philosophically while showing that oral dialectic will necessarily
go beyond what the dialogues themselves can offer. *Reading Plato*
offers a concise and illuminating insight into the complexities
and difficulties of the Platonic dialogues which will be invaluable
to any student of Plato's philosophy. Since publication of the
German original (1993) *Reading Plato* has been translated into
several European languages.

READING PLATO

Thomas A. Szlezák

Translated by Graham Zanker

London and New York

First published 1993
as *Platon lesen*
by Verlag frommann-holzboog, Stuttgart

First published in English 1999
by Routledge
11 New Fetter Lane, London EC4P 4EE

Simultaneously published in the USA and Canada
by Routledge
29 West 35th Street, New York, NY 10001

© 1993 Friedrich Frommann Verlag Günther Holzboog

Translation © 1999 Routledge

The right of Thomas A. Szlezák to be identified as the Author of this
Work has been asserted by him in accordance with the Copyright,
Designs and Patents Act 1988

Typeset in Garamond by RefineCatch Limited, Bungay, Suffolk
Printed and bound in Great Britain by
Clays Ltd, St Ives plc

British Library Cataloguing in Publication Data
A catalogue record for this book is available from the British Library

Library of Congress Cataloging in Publication Data
Szlezák, Thomas Alexander.
[Platon lesen. English]
Reading Plato/Thomas A. Szlezák; translated by Graham Zanker.
p.   cm.
Originally published: Platon lesen. Stuttgart: Verlag
frommann-holzboog, 1993.
Includes bibliographical references and index of passages.
1. Plato. Dialogues.
B395.S96913   1999
184–dc21   98–34035 CIP

ISBN 0–415–18983–7 (hbk)
ISBN 0–415–18984–5 (pbk)

For Oliver Taplin and Christopher Rowe,
remembering our time together
at the University of Bristol in 1972.

Th. A. Sz.

For the Philologisches Seminar of
Tübingen University
in gratitude

G. Z.

CONTENTS

CONTENTS

PREFACE

Plato has never lacked readers, and we need not fear that he will lack them in the future. Certainly, he does not need to be 'discovered' these days. But there is a special feature about reading him. Perhaps no other philosophical author has had such a mixed attitude to writing as a means of disseminating knowledge as Plato. The dialogue-form is rightly considered to be an extraordinarily reflective manner of dealing with the written word. But what Plato wanted to achieve with it is something which is disputed as few other things are. Thus what Aristotle once said about considering the truth in general is in some measure true of reading the works of Plato: it is partly easy, because no one entirely misses the mark, and partly difficult, because no one achieves the necessary precision.

The present volume aims to develop its theme by starting from the 'easy' material, i.e. from material in Plato which is directly accessible to us moderns and not in dispute, in order to work forward from there to the 'difficult' material, i.e. to those traits of Plato's writing of dialogues which do not correspond with our modern views of the use of writing in philosophy, and which as a consequence are most often misinterpreted or even ignored, but which nevertheless reach into the heart of Plato's conception of philosophy.

Reading Plato first appeared in an Italian translation under the title *Come leggere Platone* (Rusconi, Milan 1991, 2nd edition 1992). Originally conceived as a volume to accompany the new translation of all Plato's dialogues by Giovanni Reale and his collaborators, the book is directed not only to the Plato-specialist – though naturally to him as well – but at the same time to the non-specialist inside and outside the 'discipline' of philosophy. It does not aim to simplify or popularise, but certainly attempts to bring the complex problems of interpreting the Platonic dialogues to Plato's growing

PREFACE

readership in a form which is not only accessible to the specialist who has spent years on the task.

The aim of this work is not a detailed engagement with the Romantic paradigm of interpreting Plato, which was founded by Friedrich Schleiermacher and from which the picture sketched here of Plato's aims, methods and techniques differs in essential points: for that, the reader is referred to *Platon und die Schriftlichkeit der Philosophie* (Berlin and New York 1985) and there in particular to the appendix on method ('Die moderne Theorie der Dialogform', pp. 331–375). At the wish of the Rusconi Press references are made to this book from the start, but no knowledge of it at all is assumed for reading the present work.

The aim is to reach an interpretation of Plato's philosophical writing which can endure in the face of Plato's critique of writing in the *Phaedrus*. To want to devalue Plato's own devaluation of writing or turn it into its opposite, as has been standard practice since the Romantic period and is frequently still to this day, cannot open any path towards understanding Plato as a writer. Only if Plato's evaluation of written and spoken philosophical inquiry is taken seriously can the dialogues' technique and intention be adequately understood. Today's reader must adapt himself to the perspective of the author, against all kinds of prejudices and resistance which are specific to modern times.

It is only in this way, I believe, that we can experience the joy of reading which, for the author's part – according to a remarkable testimony of Plato about himself – is mirrored by the joy at the success of the thinker's written 'gardens of Adonis' (*Phaedrus* 276d).

Thomas Alexander Szlezák

1

THE JOY OF READING PLATO

Above everything else, reading Plato entails a unique intellectual pleasure. The joy of engaging with his thought comes not only from experiencing the artistic perfection of his philosophical dramas. There is also the sense that as a reader one is not only a witness but somehow a part of the lively discussion which Plato presents in masterly strokes as if it were a natural interaction between characters who seem to be taken from life itself.

Directness and freshness, which have been admired throughout the ages as a characteristic of Greek art and culture in general, are qualities which few, even within that culture, achieved to the degree that Plato did. Although he was the spiritual heir of the immensely creative lyric and classical ages and was able to assimilate the experience of generations of poets and thinkers in a highly reflective way, he can at the same time create the impression that philosophical inquiry began, as if without any presuppositions, from zero, in the brilliant world of Athens he portrays.

A second, equally important characteristic of his literary world is its variety and its far-reaching intellectual richness. For the directness and authenticity of his presentation of the Athenian ambience in no way mean that as a writer Plato was completely dominated by the historical events and social limits of that world alone. With the sovereign sweep of a poet, Plato connects his native Athens with everything that Greek intellectual history had produced. Certainly, in undertaking this he was able to refer to historical events, for example when he makes the great intellectuals of the fifth century BC, who indeed liked coming to Athens, appear in the early dialogues in front of an Athenian public and advertise their new systems of education. But in the later works, when he makes a 'Stranger from Elea' who remains anonymous or even Parmenides himself (in the dialogue named after him) come to Athens and talk philosophy

1

with the young Socrates, all biographical and historical plausibility is thrown aside. In the dialogue on the philosophy of nature, the *Timaeus*, a non-Athenian statesman and scholar, whom we are to imagine as a Pythagorean even if he is not explicitly described as such, speaks before a small group, of which only half are Athenians, on the topic of the structuring of the cosmos by means of the divine reason of the Demiurge; in Plato's last work, the *Laws*, by contrast, an Athenian, who on this occasion remains anonymous and thereby reflects the culture of his city all the more, is on foreign ground, namely on Crete, in the company of two representatives of the conservative culture of the Dorians, when he drafts a comprehensive picture of a well-ordered future society and its intellectual foundations.

Apparently, then, Plato intended not only to broaden the intellectual horizon from time to time by the literary device of the choice of dialogue-partner, but in general also to reflect a complex historical process: first, the new scientific and social educational systems developed outside of Athens entered the politically powerful city; here, by engaging with the intellectual wealth imported from outside, Athenian conceptual philosophy was developed which, as soon as it was sure of its methods, shaped its responses more radically and assimilated the foundations of the fifth century, the philosophies of the Eleatics, Heraclitus and the Pythagoreans; finally, such an examination of the foundations resulted, as the *Laws* symbolise, in the transmission of a politico-moral system, which had evolved from the most rigorous, methodical schooling, to the whole Hellenic world through 'the Athenian'. Thus, through the medium of the Platonic dialogue-partners from the early to the late dialogues, we pass through the historical development of Athens from intellectual receptivity to critical deepening and finally to normative creativity.

So the dialogues' directness, their variety and their capacity to serve as a symbol, of which we have already received a first impression, have established Plato as the author who is regarded everywhere today, regardless of the differences between national cultures, as the author who is most effective at awakening an interest in philosophy. Whoever begins to conduct philosophical inquiry with Plato can be sure that he or she is on the right path.

At the same time, his powers of stimulation are by no means limited to the philosopher's initial stages. The truly astonishing thing is rather that Plato not only defined the standard of what could from then on in Europe be called philosophy, but also elaborated a number of essential questions of metaphysics, epistemology, ethics and political philosophy in so fundamental a way that, in spite of such an immensely fruitful development of two and a half thousand years, it is impossible not to take account of his approaches to solutions, or at least his statement of problems.

These should therefore be the most important factors for the modern public's experience of reading Plato. The sense that we can take part in philosophy at its first and still unadulterated origins, bound together with the conviction that we are being confronted with questions of a relevance which remains undiminished, and sustained by our experiencing virtuosity in language and composition, produces for the receptive reader the sense of intellectual joy with which we began.

2

THE READER PARTICIPATES

Taken on its own, however, this experience still does not explain why the question of *how* one should read the text is debated with special passion and controversy precisely in the case of Plato. Even non-specialists have come to know that this is the case. With no other thinker does the question of the literary form in which the philosophical subject-matter is cast and, as a consequence, the question of the manner in which the reader must approach this particular form, gain so much importance as with Plato. For with no other thinker is the form of the representation so directly relevant to the subject-matter as with him; the correct understanding of the dialogue-form and the correct understanding of the Platonic conception of philosophy are interdependent. It is a paradoxical situation: this author, who is unrivalled in his ability to facilitate the experience of entering philosophical inquiry, appears to need his own specific system of hermeneutics for being understood.

It is certainly no coincidence that the interpretation of the works of Plato and the independent discipline of philosophical hermeneutics have come into very close contact with one another at two important points in their development. It was the important Romantic philosopher and theologian Friedrich Schleiermacher (1768–1834) who was the first to reflect on the active role of the reader and from this developed a method of interpreting the dialogues, the fundamentals of which many even today still regard as valid. It was also Schleiermacher who re-thought the old problem of theology concerning correct exegesis and thus advanced to a universal hermeneutics which can be regarded as the actual beginning of modern hermeneutic philosophy. And, in our own century, Hans-Georg Gadamer took his philosophical starting-point precisely from Plato and in his first work, *Platons dialektische Ethik* (1931), thereby deepened and put in concrete form Schleiermacher's pioneering insights on the meaning of form for content. Gadamer also produced, in his main work, *Wahrheit und Methode* (1960), a new foundation for philosophical hermeneutics.

The question of the correct way of reading Plato is ultimately a question of the ways in which the reader plays a part in what he or she is reading. That we cannot, when reading, abstract ourselves from our own ego, that we cannot annul our manifold limitations and that as a consequence we ourselves form a vital factor in the process of reading is a datum which is valid for every kind of reading and is accepted by everyone. With Plato, however, there is the additional fact that, as we noticed at the outset, the reader almost inevitably gets the feeling not only of being a witness but in some scarcely definable way also of being part of the argument which he is following – which must also have consequences for the way in which he responds to the content. And, inasmuch as the deep-seated, personal participation in the dialogue is obviously not an effect which is merely accidental in the works of Plato or in any way against the author's intention, the problem with which we are confronted here cannot simply be one of eliminating as extensively as possible all subjective elements in our reception of the texts. Certainly, the aim is to be able to orientate oneself by the subject itself alone (see *Phaedo* 91c); but as long as one is still only on the way toward this aim, it would not be helpful to act as if it were already achieved and on that basis to eliminate the possibility that decisive hindrances (but in favourable cases aids as well) may exist within ourselves for approaching the aim. Obviously, we should react to Plato's dramas with our entire being and not only with our analytical reasoning. The question is therefore what form the active participation of the reader should take and what part his spontaneous contribution may have in the construction of meaning.

3

AN EXAMPLE OF INDIVIDUAL RECEPTION

Nobody was more conscious than Plato that the reception of philosophy is conditioned by each individual's limitations. Again and again he makes us experience how an interlocutor is hindered by his own particular mind-set from grasping what is meant.

One of the most famous examples is Callicles in the dialogue, the *Gorgias*. Callicles represents the thesis of the so-called natural right of the stronger. According to this it is right and proper that the man who is superior to the others in strength and power subjugate them and ruthlessly use them for the furtherance of his own interests. The thesis goes that nature itself desires the dominance of the stronger; the traditional view of justice, which limits the fulfilment of one's own desires in terms of the rights of others, is nothing other than an ideological construct of the weak by means of which, for their self-protection, they wish to discredit the strong man's healthy striving after the uninhibited fulfilment of his instincts and wishes (see *Gorgias* 482c–486d).

Plato could have had this thesis debated in a calm and disassociated manner as a simply theoretical contribution towards a basic foundation of ethics. Instead, he makes Callicles express it as his own peronal belief. It is not just an intellectual 'position' but the direct expression of his pathological ambition and his boundless egocentrism. When Socrates demonstrates to him with compelling reasons that the conventional concept of justice makes sense while the so-called right of the stronger is self-contradictory, Callicles can no longer follow Socrates' reasoning – certainly not, however, out of a lack of intelligence, because he obviously has no little of that, but because of the limitations of his character. It is stated quite openly that it is his unbridled drives which hinder him from understanding and accepting Socrates' theoretically well founded and morally wholesome view (see *Gorgias* 513c).

In particular, Callicles has a perverted view of himself: he identifies himself with his desires and instincts (*Gorgias* 491e–492c). He does not know and does not want to know that human beings are more than their instincts and that reason does not exist in them to be deployed purely instrumentally in the service of their instincts, but is a divine force which exercises control over the lower parts of the soul. Socrates obviously has a corresponding theory of the inner structure of man available as a reply (see *Gorgias* 493aff.), but when he sees that Callicles would not be able to know what to make of it, he does not even begin to explain it with arguments, but is content to give a few hints which are only understandable in their full range from the fully developed doctrine of the soul in the *Republic*. Callicles is, however, made aware that he still does not know even the 'Lesser Mysteries'; but initiation into the 'Greater Mysteries' is not permissible without a knowledge of the lower step (497c). Put another way, the real solution of the problem, which for Plato can be produced only by recourse to the inner structure of man, does not need to be imparted to a character like Callicles, since he lacks the personal qualifications for accepting such truths adequately.[1] Thus Callicles receives only an *ad hominem* refutation as Socrates demonstrates the contradictory nature of his position, on Callicles' own level of argumentation (494bff.).

With this brilliant example of literary characterisation Plato tells us with all clarity that his philosophy demands the whole human being. Intellectual capability alone is insufficient; what is required is an inner relationship between the thing which is to be conveyed and the soul to which it is to be conveyed. Anybody who is not prepared to enter upon a process of inner transformation is not entitled to know the full solution either.

But a positive attitude is needed not only towards the case which the philosopher presents. Because philosophical inquiry is a process which goes on between individual human beings, good will (εὔνοια) toward one's partner is also necessary. Plato shows in a very striking way that the conversation between Socrates and Callicles ceases to be real communication because Callicles cannot meet his partner with good will.[2] In fact it is Plato's conviction that real philosophical inquiry is only possible among friends, and that philosophical argumentation, if it is to be productive in real terms, can be conducted only in 'well-intentioned refutations' (εὐμενέσιν ἐλέγχοις, *Letter* 7, 344b5). This conviction, which determines Plato's character-depiction in all dialogues, is discernible with particular clarity – apart from the *Gorgias* – in for example the *Lysis*, the

Symposium, the *Phaedrus* and the *Republic*. Indeed, 'friendship' is not to be understood in this connection as subjective, random inclination, and thus as a mere emotion, but follows from the shared orientation towards the 'divine' and the 'eternally existent', and in the final analysis towards the idea of the Good itself.

Callicles is certainly an extreme character. Plato has drawn him, in all his ruthlessly open profession of immorality, with intentional provocativeness – as a provocation directed at philosophical opponents who disapprove of his foundation of ethics in a metaphysical doctrine of the soul and the Ideas, but also as a provocation directed at the future reader – to us, then, who all have in ourselves a Callicles, at least potentially. The challengingly true-to-life portrait of a basic hostility to ethics compels us to clarify our attitude to the 'right of the stronger' – our conscious attitude and even more our unconscious one.

4

POSSIBLE MISTAKEN
ATTITUDES ON THE PART OF
THE READER

While good will towards one's discussion-partner is necessary for any genuine understanding, for us as readers the live opposite number is replaced by written depiction. Reaching a correct attitude is undoubtedly made difficult by this, inasmuch as any wrong attitudes which may crop up cannot be corrected by the book, in contrast with when one is dealing with a personal partner. It is thus of decisive importance that certain irritations which might be experienced when reading Plato should be recognised as such and counteracted. It should be remembered that here we are dealing with irritations which we know by experience may be felt by a reader who is basically open-minded and interested in philosophy, who in addition has taste and education. It has to be realised that these are a consequence of Plato's conception of the correct manner of philosophical communication, and are thus in the final analysis a consequence of his concept of philosophy; only in this way can we avoid letting passing irritations become a lasting obstacle to assimilating Plato's thought.

(a) In the aporetic dialogues, whenever a solution is not reached after a long, vain search even at the last attempt, the reader, for whom the point of the strange, aimless journey remains concealed, easily gets the impression that the whole process has been just an idle exercise, or at any rate is a prelude far too extended for fruitful philosophical inquiry, which meanwhile has not yet eventuated.

(b) In the constructive dialogues, whenever it is said of the most essential problems that they cannot be discussed 'now' or that they must be tackled on another occasion, one impatiently asks oneself why such rewarding themes are, as it were, only paraded before us and immediately removed again, and whether there was anything at all in Plato's thought which corresponded with this continual foreshadowing of even more essential material, or whether the reader is turned into a Tantalus who is merely made to believe that real fruit is present.

(c) Finally, common to the early and later dialogues is the unshakable superiority of the leader of the discussion over any given partner. One might accept that the Athenian in the *Laws* is instructing his inexperienced Dorian friends unrelentingly from an inexhaustible supply of superior knowledge, or that the Stranger from Elea has a considerable advantage over the young people with whom he is conversing; but in the dialogues of an agonistic type the dictates of fairness seem violated when the interlocutors are all too unequal and Socrates apparently never has any trouble in triumphing over his opponents. One asks in disbelief whether such a towering champion in verbal debate could exist who could throw everyone with the same ease, whether it is the all-rounder Hippias, the radical Callicles, the irritable Thrasymachus or even the celebrated Protagoras and the highly respected Gorgias. Somehow that seems unlikely, scarcely even credible; instinctively one wishes for a greater balance, a greater equality, and indeed many an annoyed reader might inwardly start opposing the invincible Socrates.

Such reactions are completely understandable. But they only have to be seen in their context for it to become clear that they are a matter of our typically modern desire for equality and unrestricted exposure of suspected hidden agendas. As people of the democratic, pluralist and anti-authoritarian twentieth century we are, whether we know it or not, emotionally so attuned to the prevalent relativism that, confronted with a monumentally superior Socrates or Athenian who is so bold as to describe the orientation he represents as the only correct one, we meet them with scepticism or inner resistance, and feel their play with aporia to be a lack of openness, and their reference to insights to be won in the future to be an avoidance of the demands of the moment. Instead, we should be asking ourselves whether Plato does not want to communicate something special, something no longer directly understandable to us by conceiving his characters in such a way, and whether this does not perhaps refer to a concept of philosophy which is fundamentally different from twentieth-century values, but for that very reason capable of complementing and enriching them.

From this we see that, by the same token, the reader's total and not only intellectual reaction to the events of the dialogues, which is provoked by the text itself, conceals a danger. Anybody who fails to detect the distorting factor which he himself represents runs the danger of getting stuck in a reading which is superficial. The distorting element does not have to be of a purely individual or subjective kind. It is not only individuals who play a part in what they are reading but whole epochs. That can lead to a situation where things in the text are not seen or noticed for generations, simply because they do not fit into the thought of the period. The example which follows will illustrate this.

5

ONE DOES NOT SEE WHAT ONE DOES NOT KNOW

(a) The motif of 'concealment' in the dialogues

Since Schleiermacher's discovery that for Plato form is not inessential for content, the interpretation of Plato has been faced with the task of examining the dialogues' dramatic technique both as a whole and in individual detail. Unfortunately, it cannot be said that research has made much progress in completing this task. Nevertheless, particular dramaturgical techniques, like the change of interlocutor, and particular recurrent motifs, like the appeal to sayings of poets, have been described repeatedly. But one motif has remained as good as disregarded, although it should have warranted precise description and interpretation on the grounds of its peculiarity and its need of explanation, but above all on the grounds of its prominence in Plato's works. I mean the motif of concealment and the intentional withholding of knowledge.

To us, this motif is peculiar because in the West the postulate that the fruits of philosophical and scholarly labour be accorded unrestricted publication has prevailed for a long time, and consequently no one even countenances the possibility that anyone could consciously withhold a conclusion worthy of mention. (Let us however bear in mind that it was only in the seventeenth century, and with considerable difficulty, that the idea of the basic openness of intellectual work was accepted, as the American sociologist Robert K. Merton has proved;[3] to ascribe this attitude, as if it were a natural one, to earlier epochs would thus be naive, because it is ahistorical.)

As for the frequency of the motif of concealment, it is truly astonishing to see how regularly Plato has recourse to it. Again and again, Socrates' discussion-partners fall under suspicion of not wanting to reveal their knowledge or not completely, whether it is simply to

12

keep it for themselves, as appears to be the case with the Heraclitean Cratylus and the eccentric, would-be theologian Euthyphro, or also to test the others, as is imputed to the sophist Prodicus, or even to cheat them, as is regarded as possible for Critias, Callicles, Hippias and Ion the rhapsode.[4] In these cases it might to some extent be excusable that the motif which is obviously important to Plato has not received appropriate attention. But it seems truly unbelievable that no one has noticed that in one of the formally most perfect dialogues, the *Euthydemus*, withholding knowledge shapes the structure and also extensively defines the meaning, as a motif without an understanding of which the meaning of the whole dialogue can be grasped only incompletely. The 'plot' of the *Euthydemus* consists of Socrates' attempt to induce the sophists Euthydemus and Dionysodorus to drop their frivolous antics and conundrums for once, and to display what they can contribute in terms of serious philosophy. So Socrates implies that they have important insights at their disposal, but have been intentionally withholding them up till now. When he has no success in teasing out the serious side of the sophists, he recommends to them that they should not deal with their wisdom too lavishly in the future either, but to remain as sparing with it as they have been up till now, for, as he puts it, 'What is rare has value' (*Euthydemus* 304b: how to interpret Socrates' conduct is something which will concern us directly).

Conscious withholding of philosophical knowledge is something which Plato envisages not only as a possible decision of individual people but also as a measure by the state for organizing education. Even in the relatively early *Protagoras* a fictitious picture is sketched, not without humorous touches, of the 'real' Sparta, whose actual strength was not waging war but philosophical inquiry. Unfortunately, the fiction continues, the rest of the Greeks knew nothing about this oldest and most important source of philosophy in Greece because the Spartans did not let them participate, but either associated with their leading thinkers in secret or staged the well-known expulsions of foreigners, the real aim of which was to enable them to conduct philosophical inquiry without witnesses (*Protagoras* 342a–e).

More important than this comic fiction is the picture offered by the two political utopias. In the *Republic* the precise programme for the training of the philosophical ruling élite presupposes that the content of their education is not freely available. For example, there would simply be no sense to the regulation that only the most capable be led to the contemplation of the highest principle, the Idea of the Good, and even these only after their fiftieth year (*Republic* 540a), if the twenty-year-olds, and among them the average and weaker talents, who are to be excluded from the 'most precise education' (503d), were able to access information, for instance in written form, about the philosophical activities of the last phase. The long, arduous period of preparatory disciplines and the systematic transition, not anticipating anything, to each next higher phase is only conceivable if those who have the higher forms of knowledge at their disposal deal with it responsibly, and that means that they make it accessible only to those who are adequately equipped for it. (We shall see that Socrates himself also behaves in this spirit in the *Republic*.) In Plato's later plan of the ideal state, the *Laws*, the highest leadership of the state, the so-called 'nocturnal council', is surrounded by an aura of secrecy from the outset – the ordinary citizen of the Cretan ideal state has no access either to the decisions or to the information and the education on the basis of which the members make their decisions (*Laws* 951d–952b, 961a–b; cf. 968d–e).

(b) Socrates himself withholds knowledge

On the basis of our findings so far it can already be said with certainty that for Plato – unlike the twentieth century – the withholding of knowledge was a central idea of obviously great relevance. That becomes even clearer if we examine Socrates' conduct in the *Euthydemus*. We have just noticed that he implies that the sophists Euthydemus and Dionysodorus were intentionally offering mere 'play', behind which, however, a philosophical 'seriousness' exists, which for the time being is being concealed. His single-minded attempt, pursued through the whole dialogue, to elicit the 'serious' views of his partners shows none the less with increasing clarity that in reality they have nothing apart from the silly, fraudulent conclusions with which they cheat young people. Socrates sees through this from the beginning – his insistence on an intentionally concealed 'seriousness' behind the 'play' of the sophists is nothing other than naked irony.

But why does Socrates choose precisely this form of mockery of his opponents? A look at the philosophical theories which he himself alludes to in this dialogue, though without developing them with argumentation, can explain his behaviour: this Socrates obviously knows the Platonic doctrine of anamnesis and Ideas, including the theory of dialectic. Admittedly, the modern reader can accept this as a certainty only after a careful comparison of Socrates' statements in the *Euthydemus* with the corresponding arguments in other dialogues, particularly in the *Meno*, the *Phaedo* and the *Republic*. Only the reader who is in possession of this extended philosophical background can combine the fragmentary and abruptly interspersed allusions into a meaningful whole. The upshot for us is that, if the dialogue *Euthydemus* were the sole extant work of Plato, we would not be able to understand the philosophical point of view of the principal character in the dialogue – just as Socrates' interlocutors in the dialogue evidently cannot understand him. In other words, Socrates acts 'esoterically' in the *Euthydemus*; he possesses a deeper, reasoned knowledge, but sees no obligation to disclose this knowledge before participants in the conversation who are either inadequately trained or who are basically not suited for philosophy. The ability to withhold philosophical knowledge if necessary, when circumstances demand it, is something which Plato thus presents as a positive quality of the true philosopher. It is a biting piece of sarcasm that Socrates ascribes this positive quality, with scornful praise, to the pseudo-philosophers Euthydemus and Dionysodorus, a quality to which they evidently have absolutely no claim.[5]

Accordingly, anyone who has understood the subtle irony at play in the *Euthydemus* will not misinterpret Socrates' ridicule of concealment here and in other dialogues as an expression of an anti-esoteric view on Plato's part, but as a suggestion that only the true philosopher is capable of meaningful reticence, or of a mode of communication which takes into account the limits of the recipient.

The opposed position, that one displays one's knowledge, without considering the needs and degree of education of one's audience, and brings it to market, like a storekeeper who loudly pushes his wares and tries to sell them to as many as possible, is, in Plato's opinion, the position of the sophist. The sophist, in his very essence, is antiesoteric. It is no surprise that Plato makes none other than Protagoras, the most important leader of the fifth-century sophistic movement, express a plea for basic openness in the communication of knowledge (*Protagoras* 317b–c).

(c) The dialogues point beyond themselves

How little it would suit Socrates as the literary ideal philosopher-figure to dispense his knowledge indiscriminately is also demonstrated by the dialogues *Charmides* and the *Republic*, along with many other examples.[6] In the extended framing action of the

Charmides, the subject of discussion is, in a transparent metaphor, a medication (φάρμακον) imported from Thrace which Socrates could give to the young Charmides to heal his headache – but he does not give it to him since it would only be of use to someone who, Socrates adds, first exposed his soul to the charm (*Charmides* 155e). The medication, therefore, is ready for use here too, but is deliberately not applied, because the recipient is philosophically not yet advanced enough to receive it to any good effect.

In the *Republic* the continuous 'plot' consists of the attempt of the brothers Glaucon and Adeimantus to induce Socrates to impart his views on justice. Despite his esteem for the brothers, this is not a foregone conclusion for him; instead, again and again a new 'coercion' is needed to get Socrates to reveal more of his views. Now it is crucial that the 'coercion' which Glaucon and Adeimantus exert is successful only up to a certain point: indeed, Socrates sketches the picture of an ideal state in the course of which he also says what justice consists of; but, when he is pressed to explain his views on the Idea of the Good as the principle of all things more precisely, he declares that he is disregarding a great deal, and in particular what is most essential, namely the discussion of the 'nature' (the τί ἐστιν) of the Good (509c with 506d–e). And when Glaucon insists again at a later juncture and wants to know something more precise about the philosophical dialectic which Socrates has only sketched in out-line, Socrates even informs him of the reason why he intentionally limits his communication of philosophy: he himself, Glaucon, is the reason, inasmuch as he is intellectually not equal to the more precise arguments for which Socrates is capable and ready (*Republic* 533a). With this example we have already touched a central structural characteristic of the Platonic dialogues: it is not only the *Republic* which uses passages like the ones described, but almost all dialogues present, at some structurally emphatic point, one or more state-ments in which the discussion-leader makes it unmistakably clear that he has other more important things to say about precisely the most essential aspects of the subject being treated, but will not do it there and then. These passages, which are of the greatest importance for the correct understanding of Plato and which will repeatedly continue to occupy our attention, we shall designate in what follows as 'deliberate gaps', to be 'filled in', either in another dialogue or by further oral discussion, on some other occasion.

Modern interpretations of Plato during the most recent gener-ations have paid scarcely any attention to the features that I have described in the preceding pages – the recurrent insinuation that the

interlocutors will withhold knowledge; Plato's elucidation of the
meaning of this motif by means of the 'plot' of the *Euthydemus*;
the limited access to philosophy in the outlines of the ideal state; the
plot of all the dialogues which exhibit, through Socrates himself, a
strictly addressee-directed, i.e. 'esoteric', handling of philosophical
communication; and, finally, even the explicit evidence of the 'gaps'.
They have either not even been noticed, as with Socrates' subtle play
with the reproach of 'esotericism', or they have been, as with the
'deliberate gaps', only partially understood and systematically
misinterpreted as the consequence of such a narrowing of vision.[7]

The reason for this is, as has already been hinted, that our whole
epoch, 'modernity' since the Enlightenment as well as so-called
post-modernity, has no use for the conscious limitation of philosophical communication and consequently has no comprehension of
it. One sees only what one knows.

Plato did not write for the book-culture of the nineteenth and
twentieth centuries. If we do not start taking this simple but fundamental insight seriously, we cut ourselves off from access to his
philosophical intention.

The consideration of Plato's criticism of literacy in the *Phaedrus*
will make his attitude to the problem of communicating philosophical knowledge comprehensible (below, Ch. 12). Before we
come to that we must attempt a stock-taking of the Platonic dialogues' essential formal characteristics (which are, however, at the
same time relevant to content) (Chs 6 and 7), and ask ourselves
whether we can ascertain what audience Plato was actually writing
for (Ch. 8) and whether he is committed to a particular theory of
interpreting texts and writes with it in view (Chs 9 and 10).

6

CHARACTERISTICS OF THE PLATONIC DIALOGUES

The following observations are an attempt to understand the essential characteristics which together provide the basic outlines of a morphology of Plato's dialogues. Taken together, these characteristics are the expression of a particular approach to communicating philosophical knowledge, and thus also indirectly of a particular concept of philosophy.

Only those characteristics are considered to which there is no exception, or almost none, and which are to be found in all phases of Plato's *œuvre* (which is why, for example, the aporetic ending, which is typical of some of the earlier works, has not been included). Every theory of Plato's dialogues should be able to explain such fundamental characteristics; surprisingly, however, as must now be emphasised, the antiesoteric theory of the dialogues which has prevailed in the nineteenth and twentieth centuries can offer only a partial explanation for these characteristics – a clear indication that it must be replaced by a new paradigm which comes closer to Plato's convictions.

1   The philosophical works of Plato depict, without exception, *conversations*. However, within the framework of the conversation long *monologues* are also possible.
2   The conversation takes place in a particular place and at a particular time. The participants are personages who are characterised in a way which is true to life, persons who are with few exceptions historically verifiable.
3   Each dialogue has a figure who clearly takes over the leadership in the conversation. The name of the leader in the conversation is pre-eminently Socrates; he is individually characterised like the other participants, though admittedly from the very beginning with a certain idealising tendency. In the later dialogues the

discussion-leader can have other names as well; in these cases he remains less clear as a person than the other interlocutors.

4   The discussion-leader speaks in each case only with one partner. Conversations with more than two participants fall into sections of conversation which show the leader in discussion with changing partners. Three-party conversations on a larger scale do not exist. The leader can suspend the conversation with his real partner and replace it by a model dialogue with an imaginary partner.

5   The discussion-leader can answer all objections. In conversations of an agonistic character he can refute all participants; he himself never is refuted. All elements of the conversation which are really helpful ones are introduced by him (sometimes, indeed, in a 'maieutic' manner: he brings to light 'somebody else's' thoughts).

6   The conversation does not grow more intense in a continuous fashion but is raised almost jerkily on to a qualitatively higher stage, most often in the course of warding off an attack.

7   The discussion-leader does not bring the argumentation to an organic conclusion, but refers to future themes, topics requiring proof, areas for further work, a discussion of which would be necessary in the light of the particular subject itself, but which he describes as lying outside the range of the present investigation. Every Platonic dialogue has its 'deliberate gap' or 'gaps'.

7

QUESTIONS ABOUT THE CHARACTERISTICS

The most obvious of these characteristics of Plato's works have generally been interpreted too readily in the spirit of our age's current thought-patterns. Because scholars have thought that in this way they already have the correct answers, they have again and again failed to ask the really essential questions of the evidence of the dialogues themselves. In what follows, let me enumerate some of the usual misunderstandings, which we must avoid, together with the most important questions that emerge when we consider the list of characteristics.

On (1): Is philosophical inquiry possible for Plato only in dialogue-form? Is it bound to 'existential communication' (in the sense of twentieth-century existentialism), and is the dialogue-form the only conceivable legitimate mode of depicting philosophy?

Care is needed here. We should not forget that, in the very dialogue in which Plato makes Socrates plead with particular vigour against the sophists' 'long speech' (μακρὸς λόγος, makros logos) and on behalf of the question-and-answer process, namely in the *Protagoras*, Plato simultaneously displays a Socrates who himself gives a long discourse in continuous speech (342a–347a) and, furthermore, defers the live argument with Protagoras for the time being in favour of an imaginary discussion (on this artistic technique of Plato's see below, on point 4). In terms of content, therefore, the result that Socrates reaches is not dependent on Protagoras' answer to him.[8] That is also confirmed by Plato's occasional depiction of him as the lonely meditator, or by Plato's making him refer back to alleged earlier agreements and discussions or to pieces of instruction which he claims to have received from third parties:[9] all of this clearly shows that it is far from the discussion-leader's intentions to work out everything here and now; rather, he brings essential modes of thought and conclusions ready-made into the discussion. That should warn us against naive hymns to 'the dialogical' and the 'live process of discussion'. The importance of the dialogical nature of thinking is not thereby denied. But the real point at issue is the process of dialogue in *thought* inasmuch as thought is, according to Plato, a conversation of the soul with itself.[10] Whatever is discovered through thinking on one's own must be verifiable in conversation with others; Socrates describes it as a general necessity to submit one's discovery to others and confirm it with them.[11] Yet what matters primarily is *basic* verifiability, and when Socrates attaches importance to checking everything with the *best* questioner and answerer, as he asserts in the *Protagoras*, he is none the less forced to resort to his own thinking rather than Protagoras'. But an account which is not dialogical in terms of form can also satisfy the basic dialogical nature of thinking. This is shown with adequate clarity by the sections in the *œuvre* of Plato which are not turned into dialogue-form, among which we can count the fifth book and large parts of the sixth book of the *Laws*, the Eros-speech in the *Phaedrus* and above all the magnificent monologue of the title-figure in the *Timaeus*: all that is as much a genuine expression of Platonic philosophy as progressing in short questions and even shorter answers.

Nor should Plato's use of the dialogue-form mislead us into believing that he wanted to remain 'anonymous', to hide behind the views of his fictitious characters. However widespread the belief in Plato's 'anonymity' may be and however respected the scholars who represent it,[12] it is nothing more than a rather naive misunderstanding. At first it might indeed seem quite a subtle consideration to notice that Plato nowhere speaks in his own name but merely dramatises the conflict of the opinions of others. However, from here to intentional anonymity is a large step. A philosopher who really remained anonymous for some time was Søren Kierkegaard, who represented opposed views under various pseudonyms like Climacus and Anticlimacus; anybody who at all realised that one anonymous author alone stood behind these views could indeed ask himself in confusion what the real view of the author was. Nothing of the kind happens in the case of Plato: nowhere is it recorded that at any time he had any of his works circulated under a false name, and it was at most in the aporetic dialogues that it remained partially unclear what he really thought (though these dialogues also are often very clear in their negative results). For example, that Plato himself also believed in the immortality of the soul even when he makes 'only'

Socrates, Timaeus and the Athenian argue for this view is something which no reader in antiquity doubted, and we too would be displaying pretty unsubtle powers of judgment if we wanted to doubt it today.

On (2): Pinning down the frame of the dialogues to a definite place and a definite time, as well as introducing individual, historical characters, is a strong indication that entering philosophical inquiry can only succeed at any time with personal effort. One could misinterpret all this as emphasising that the results arrived at are conditioned by Plato's times – certainly, there is the view that Plato believed that the philosopher has 'nothing to express that he would not immediately question.' To put this belief into effect Plato could indeed have radically relativised the truth which was being sought after precisely through individualising and personalising the course of the conversation.

First, however, Plato never held this view, and, second, it should be stressed that the 'historicity' of the situations and figures of the dialogues is a historicity which is tempered with the greatest poetic licence. For the partners in the dialogues as well as for the reader, the aim is to shake off the chains of their individuality and to advance to abiding truths. The dependence of the dialogues on a particular situation and time is thus an 'ideal' or exemplary one. It is only for this reason that we can recognise our own conditioning in it. If Plato's figures were *only* historical figures, they would not be able to touch us as closely as they in fact do. Fortunately, they are not individual in a merely historical or random way, but – if I may put it thus – individual in a generally valid way.

On (3): Doubtless it would have been a real possibility for Plato to confront Socrates or any other discussion-leader with partners who were their equals in intellect and character or conversely to depict Socrates and the other dialecticians as less superior. Strangely, the lack of a conversation among equals has rarely even been noticed, and even more rarely perceived as a problem. We shall not be able to ignore this question: it is integrally related to the question of why the discussion-leader is either idealised or characterised only in a vague way, and both questions relate in turn to Plato's conception of communicating philosophical knowledge. With partners of equal strength Plato could have left fundamental questions unsolved in a definitive way; such *radically* aporetic conclusions do not exist in Plato, as is well known (the aporetic conclusions of the early dialogues are on the other hand never the product of positions of equal strength and, over and above this, are resolved in the *Republic*). We shall have to ask what concept of philosophy is presupposed by the conception of unequal partners.

On (4): The avoidance of three-party conversations means that each participant stays focused exclusively on the discussion-leader and is corrected by him – other points of view cannot become fruitful through contact with one another. If the argument over a point of view cannot be continued with sufficient profit through the partner concerned, the discussion-leader can pass over the practical limit of the possible with sovereign style and continue the argumentation with imaginary partners. Such imaginary partners are, for instance, the atheists in the tenth book of the *Laws*, Diotima in the *Symposium*, or Socrates' anonymous house-mate in the *Hippias Maior*. The last two examples show in addition how the 'historical' character of the discussion-leader can be extended quite arbitrarily.

On (5): Plato's decision to leave the leading role in a conversation to only one figure would still not make it imperative also to equip this figure with such an advantage over the others that he is superior to them in *every* situation. That is so difficult to reconcile with modern notions of equality that it has simply been denied that Plato wishes to present Socrates as invincible in argumentation. It is, once again, more profitable to ask what conception of philosophy is expressed by this dramaturgical decision than to deny the facts.

On (6) and (7): The significance of an attack on a result that has been arrived at, which is followed by a specifically directed means of 'support' which confirms this result on a higher level by means of more advanced conceptual tools and more penetrating proofs, is made clear only when we consider the critique of writing at the end of the *Phaedrus*. Since this essential text has so far not been made the key to describing the structure of the Platonic dialogues,[13] the abrupt elevation of the level of argumentation, which a few commentators have at least noticed, has likewise never been correctly interpreted as an expression of Plato's demand that the philosopher must be one step ahead of his logos.

The Platonic discussion-leader can on purpose conduct philosophical inquiry on different levels – it depends on the partner, his needs and capacity for comprehending what level Socrates chooses. He does not pass over to a higher level without reason: true philosophy does not offer itself to interested parties of its own accord, but wishes to be sought out. Since this has not been understood (instead, there has been a tendency to imagine an allegedly pushy Socrates who philosophised with everybody on the street), it has consequently not been understood either why the author consciously limits the ascent – the 'gaps', as mentioned above, have neither been described correctly nor has anyone recognised their function, which in the final analysis consists of referring beyond what is written to Plato's oral philosophy.

8

FOR WHOM IS PLATO WRITING?

It would be of the greatest value for our critical examination of the list of characteristics if we could say for certain what public Plato was writing for. In addressing this question we are not merely following the appeal of the trend in literary scholarship which calls itself 'reception-aesthetics' (and which simply continues Classical Studies' old aim to show the needs and expectations of the original audience as a formative factor in the development and shaping of literature). Rather, the observations we have made so far have already repeatedly led us to the fact that Plato was quite aware of the significance of the differing ways philosophical subject-matter might be received. Did this awareness lead him to decide upon a specific readership?

There is no binding statement of Plato's on this question, and none was to be expected in view of his decision to give his portrayal the form of continuous dramatisation. Thus we are dependent upon inferences from the dialogues' content and tone.

Yet the picture offered by the dialogues is not at all uniform in this respect. At one end of the broad spectrum of possibilities stands the little dialogue, the *Crito*: with its moving personification of the laws which urge Socrates to remain obedient to his mother-city and with its lack of sophisticated argumentation, it seems written primarily for the philosophical layman who is predisposed to loyalty. The *Timaeus* could be placed at the other end: it offers not only a profound doctrine of the principles of nature, but also, in its second part, highly specialised findings from various scientific disciplines; it is evident that such a work is based on systematic preliminary studies and a thorough knowledge of the literature on the subjects and is most likely to have been accorded an appropriate reception by the specialist or by interested people trained in the subject. The abandonment of the dialogue-format and the in part intentionally obscure style of expression demand of the reader considerable stamina. Perseverance and the greatest acumen are also demanded by the second part of the *Parmenides*, which is indeed played out in questions and answers but, as a consequence of its rigorous concentration on the logic of the abstract concepts 'One' and 'Many', deliberately forfeits the charm and liveliness which are otherwise characteristic of Plato.

This second part of the *Parmenides* can be understood as an 'exercise' (γυμνασία, *Parmenides* 135d7), for which the youngest and most uncomplicated person among the people present is chosen as a partner of the discussion-leader (137b–c). Young adepts of philosophy are also the discussion-partners in the late dialogues *Theaetetus*, *Sophist*, *Politicus* and *Philebus* whose discussions have, in comparison with the earlier dialogues, something professionally didactic about them. The element of the methodical exercise is also emphasised in these works (see e.g. *Politicus* 285c–287a, μελέτη 'exercise', 286b1).

From the addressees of the questions *within* the dialogues one could infer the addressees of the dialogues themselves; in that case, the dialogues would have been written primarily for students of the Academy as exercise-textbooks or as the basis of their discussions. Because of their training in Platonic philosophy the students were certainly in the position to solve the text's puzzles and aporias and to supplement the missing proofs. The dialogues' references beyond themselves would in this way be brought into line with an assumed procedure in the Academy's teaching of philosophy, or even be explained by it. There is no room for doubt that on this assumption we would have a meaningful reading of at least the early aporetic dialogues.[14]

So far it seems as if we have three groups of addressees to reckon with: laymen, people with scholarly training, and Plato's students in the Academy. At the same time it would be rather arbitrary to want to separate these groups strictly from one another. Anyone who had just entered the Academy will hardly have been different from the philosophically interested layman in terms of the state of his education; on the other hand, in view of the intensity with which scientific studies were pursued in the Academy, we can imagine a gifted 'student' being a 'specialist' in one field or another after only a relatively short period. And let us not forget: no dialogue is without interest for the reader who is philosophically advanced, just as, conversely, none is so inaccessible[15] that it could not be read with profit even by a beginner.

In the *Phaedrus* Plato explains that the value of the best written works (which on the whole do not 'merit much serious attention' (Hackforth)) lies in their function as a mnemonic for the knowledgeable man (*Phaedrus* 278a1); the philosopher writes as a game and to set up an *aide-mémoire* for his old age – for himself and for everyone who follows the same path (276d1–4). Who are these people who follow the same trail as Plato? Can they be narrowed down to the students in the Academy? Let us assume for the moment that the dialogues were indeed primarily 'exercise-books for use in teaching' – would it follow from this that they were 'not intended as literature for a wide public'?[16] But Plato of all people knew that, once written, a book can be circulated indiscriminately among the most diverse readers (*Phaedrus* 275e) – he would have had to take measures to stop his writings being circulated if he had wanted to avoid a wide readership. In the writings of Isocrates, however, we have contemporary evidence that Plato's works were read outside the Academy as well, and the ambitious literary form of masterpieces like the *Phaedo* and the *Symposium*, the *Euthydemus* and the *Phaedrus* make it as good as certain that they were written for a public educated in literature also. On the other hand, the political aspects of works like the *Apology*, the *Meno*, the *Gorgias* and the *Republic* can hardly be adequately explained on the assumption that they were exclusively intended for the younger people in the community of like-minded spirits. Finally, we should remember the strong proselytising ('protreptic') effect which is felt in Plato's early and middle work and can still be perceived in many passages in the late work: it is aimed above all at the outsider who has yet to turn to philosophy.

Thus, despite the widely diverse intellectual demands which the individual dialogues present, the educated public turns out to be the primary audience at which Plato aims. No group from this public can be excluded with certainty. To put it more simply, Plato writes for everyone.

9

DOES A PLATONIC DIALOGUE SPEAK WITH SEVERAL VOICES?

The modern theory of the dialogues

Thus, as we have seen, Plato knew that a book once published can reach readers of every kind. And he knew, to judge from the evidence of the discussion of a poem of Simonides in the *Protagoras* (which we shall examine in further detail below) that different types of readers tend to take away different things from the same text. And he intentionally wrote, in any case in the majority of his *œuvre*, for everybody.

Does it follow that his aim was specifically to address each of the various types of reader with the same text at the same time? Did he have at his disposal a literary technique which allows a writer to make one thing clear to the one set of readers and another to the others at the same time and by means of the same wording? And, if he knew of such a technique, did he intentionally use it to communicate the most essential thing that he had to say in such a way that only one particular type of reader can understand it?

The question we are dealing with is illuminated with unexpected clarity by considerations which Ludwig Wittgenstein voiced in an earlier version of the preface to his *Philosophical Notes*:[17]

> If a book is written for only a few, that will become clear by its being understood only by a few. The book must automatically separate out those who understand it and those who do not. . . . If you don't want certain people to go into a room, hang a lock in front of it to which they have no key. But it's pointless to talk with them about the room unless you want them to admire it from outside! For decency's

sake, put on the door a lock which catches the eye only of those who can open it, and doesn't do so to the others.

Wittgenstein thus considers it possible and at the same time obligatory for the author to supply his text with a 'lock' which from the outset is seen only by certain readers and then can also be opened by them. By means of this 'lock' Wittgenstein expects an 'automatic separation' of readers into those who understand the book and those who do not.

Wittgenstein was not at all thinking of Plato in these considerations. But more than 100 years before he wrote them a theory of the Platonic dialogue had existed which ascribed to Plato the intention of an 'automatic separation' of readers by means of the book, and promised to make the lock he had hung in front of his dialogues conspicuous and to open it. I mean the theory, already mentioned several times, which had been propounded by Friedrich Schleiermacher, and which we can also call the 'modern theory of the Platonic dialogues', since, in its main ideas, it has received the widest currency in the nineteenth and twentieth centuries.

According to this theory the dialogues can seek out their readers by themselves, since they can automatically hold off inappropriate readers. They do not say the same thing all the time, since they reveal new levels of meaning with each re-reading and in this way answer the appropriate reader's questions. In this sense the Platonic dialogues can also defend themselves on their own against attacks, since the attacks of the non-comprehending do not reach their deeper level of meaning at all, but the doubts of the reader who can understand are dispelled by means of the more recent 'answers'. According to this theory, these capabilities make a Platonic dialogue an 'active' text, a 'partner' with whom the reader must seek out the 'conversation'.

Let us recall to begin with that the positive capacities thus found in the 'active' dialogue-book are gained by denying the failings which Plato in the *Phaedrus* ascribes to writing (γραφή) in general. Writing, says Plato, always says the same thing, cannot answer questions, cannot choose its readers by itself and cannot defend itself against attacks (*Phaedrus* 275d–e). Nowhere does Plato say that a type of written presentation exists or could exist in the future by means of which these basic failings of writing might be overcome. Only *oral* philosophical inquiry is unaffected by these failings: in live conversation the 'person with knowledge' can seek out the appropriate partner by himself; he will be able to give to questions answers which are not always the same word-for-word and he can defend himself against objections (276a, e).

The modern theory's belief that the written Platonic dialogues can achieve basically the same as 'the living and animate [i.e. oral] speech of the person with knowledge' (*Phaedrus* 276a8), and are therefore designed by Plato also to cover the same range as his oral philosophical discussion cannot be supported by proof in the text of Plato, either in the *Phaedrus* or anywhere else. The view that the dialogue is the only form of writing which overcomes its character as a book[18] is a radical step beyond Plato, and we must examine its justification in what follows.

Before we begin the examination, two observations must be made to give a general description of this theory.

(1) From the beginning, the modern theory of the dialogue-form has always had an anti-esoteric objective, which it has preserved till today. Before Schleiermacher, W.G. Tennenmann had, in his *System der platonischen Philosophie* (2 vols (Leipzig 1792–95)), propounded the view that it was never Plato's intention to depict his philosophy entirely in written form. Against this view, Schleiermacher[19] developed the conception of the dialogue as a means of depiction which in the final analysis was equal to oral conversation and thus had the intention of representing Plato's philosophy completely, if not through direct, then through indirect, communication. Since Schleiermacher 'indirect communication' has generally been regarded as a literary technique which excludes esotericism. This claim is something else for us to examine separately.

(2) In view of this approach, the modern theory of the dialogues can be described as the 'anti-esoteric interpretation of Plato' and in this regard it can be opposed to the 'esoteric interpretation' which in our century has been represented by Léon Robin, Paul Wilpert, Hans Krämer and Konrad Gaiser. Unfortunately, this opposition is like-wise misleading. For Schleiermacher did not do away with and over-come Platonic esotericism at all, but only – in accord with a general trend of German Romanticism – internalised it, transferring it to within the recipient, or, in his own words, made it into a 'property of the reader'. Even Schleiermacher and his successors share with the 'esotericists' the view that it was far from Plato's purpose to offer everything which mattered to him to everyone, undisguised. They merely dispute that Plato intentionally limited his communication of philosophy, and affirm that all that is essential is present in the written works, only veiled by the techniques of indirect communica-tion. It is left to the reader to become a 'true hearer of what lies

within' (Schleiermacher), or, to use the image of Wittgenstein, to see the 'lock' and to open it. The result is a point of view which can correctly be described only as 'esotericism inherent in the dialogue'. It is also definitive for this position that 'appropriate' and 'inappropriate' recipients are separated to the exclusion of the latter, except that according to this position the separation, which constitutes 'esotericism', occurs 'automatically' through the book itself.

Accordingly, we do not have to choose between 'anti-esoteric' and 'esoteric' interpretations of Plato, but between two forms of esotericism: in opposition to esotericism inherent within the text – it could also be called 'hermeneutic' esotericism – we have the esotericism which points beyond the dialogue, or the 'historical' esotericism: it is based on the historical reality of a doctrine of principles which was never set down in writing – the doctrine of principles which Aristotle prefers to cite in his criticism of Plato in the *Metaphysics*.

In order to make a well-informed decision between these two positions it will be necessary to cover ancient theories of multiple levels of meaning conveyed in writing, to review Plato's attitude to them and in particular to consider his critique of writing more closely (below, Chs 10 and 12). But our observations so far do not leave us completely without criteria in this question.

It is striking that the modern Schleiermacherian theory of the dialogues ignores the 'gaps'. It must ignore them or play them down, because they basically do not fit into its scheme. To continue with Wittgenstein's metaphor of the 'room' and the 'lock' on its 'door',[20] it is not the reference to the presence of a 'lock' which many cannot see that would fit in with the 'gaps' (that is, not the approach which Wittgenstein explicitly denies in his own case), but rather the statement that there are other 'rooms', which the reader is not yet standing in front of. Presumably Wittgenstein would have rejected such a statement too, for he appears to believe that the only motive for discussing the limits of communication is the author's wish that the readers 'admire the room from outside'; thus he considers that it would be 'more decent' to introduce a less obvious 'lock'. Out of the same conviction, some readers also regard any esotericism as in some way offensive. However, it is very easy to see that other motives can exist than those named by Wittgenstein: Plato, for example, certainly wanted as many people as possible to enter his 'rooms', even the innermost ones, though of course not without appropriate training. On the other hand, admiring them from outside was a matter of complete indifference to him. With this attitude he could openly refer to the existence of further 'rooms' without in the least offending against Wittgenstein's 'decency'.

Second, the modern theory of the dialogues makes the communication (the *indirect* communication) of decisive insights depend exclusively on the intellectual qualities of the reader. For the discovery of a deeper, 'actual' meaning behind wording or trains of thought which seem superficial and unproblematical to others is an achievement of attention to language, logical analysis, memory and the gift of synthesis, in short an achievement of the intellect. However, in our brief glance at the framing plot of the *Charmides* (above, p. 15ff.), we have already seen that the application of the medication which Socrates possesses is made dependent on Charmides' letting his soul be exposed to a charm first, which means at this point that he is ready to acquire the virtue of 'self-restraint' (σωφροσύνη). Likewise, we have seen that Callicles in the *Gorgias* is not excluded from the 'Greater Mysteries' because of any lack of intelligence but because of the moral disposition of his character. And, finally, in the *Republic*, where Plato expresses himself quite basically about the required qualities of the 'philosophical natures', he stresses the ethical advantages no less than the intellectual ones (*Republic* 485b–487a). A theory of the communication of the 'actual' which leaves this condition completely out of account deserves to be handled with some scepticism.

10

AN ANCIENT THEORY OF
INTERPRETATION

The idea that a text might be able to speak with several or at least
two voices is by no means of only modern origin. Even in Plato's
time it was no longer new: at least the aristocratic public of a
Theognis (681f.) or Pindar (*Olympian Odes* 2.83–86) had been
acquainted with it for a long time.[21] But from the sixth century it
had been of particular importance for the interpretation of Homer.
In the course of the archaic period the epics of Homer had achieved
authoritative validity not only as aesthetic models but as a comprehensive interpretation of the human and divine world. The
philosopher-poet Xenophanes made it a byword that everybody had
'from the beginning learned from Homer'.[22] This Xenophanes was
one of the most influential of those who objected to the anthropo-
morphic image of the divine world in Homer. Cattle would make
images of the gods in the shape of cattle if they were able, he scoffed,
and horses in the shape of horses. And as far as the behaviour of these
gods was concerned, Xenophanes concluded that Homer and Hesiod
had ascribed to them everything which brought outrage and
disgrace among humans.[23] Heraclitus, another sharp critic of the
traditional theology of the poets, went so far as to say that Homer
should be banned from the festivals.[24]

But the strength of the tradition was far too great for any attempt
to get rid of it; on the other hand, the new philosophical criticism
was too plausible for the tradition to be left unaltered. The conviction prevailed – our first evidence for it is Theagenes of Rhegium[25]
in the late sixth century – that in his apparently crude stories of
betrayal, battle, jealousy and love in the world of the gods Homer
was imparting wisdom which was not accessible to superficial
understanding. The allegorical interpretation of Homer soon
became a regular component of Greek education and made a sub-
stantial contribution to the fact that Homer's position as teacher of

the Greeks did not wane for a moment after the criticism of the early philosophers but, on the contrary, grew further entrenched. In later centuries not only the Stoa but also Neoplatonism contributed to the development of this method of poetic exegesis. And, because it was not a matter of individual interpretations but of a whole method, its application to other 'theological' texts could not fail to follow. Euripides gives us an impressive example of the interpretation of the 'deeper meaning' of a myth by a priest: in the *Bacchae*, Teiresias explains to the unbelieving Pentheus what it 'actually' means that Dionysus was born from the thigh of Zeus (Euripides, *Bacchae* 272ff.). A similar exegesis, by an unknown author, of an Orphic text has been preserved on a papyrus which was found in a fourth-century BC grave.[26]

Isocrates provides evidence that this method, which was primarily a method for the exegesis of *poets*, was applied to prose-texts too. In the second part of the *Panathenaicus* (12.240ff.) he describes how the comparison he makes in the first part between Athens and Sparta, which turns out decisively in favour of Athens, is construed by one of his students as if the praise of Athens were only the surface meaning for the superficial reader, while the attentive reader would discover behind it, as Isocrates' real intention, a covert bias towards Sparta. The praise of Athens is supposed to be meant 'not on one level' (οὐχ ἁπλῶς, 12.236) but with the ulterior motive of testing whether the students have remembered the views that their teacher had expressed before and have absorbed the speech in a spirit of philosophical inquiry.[27] To be able to write in such a way, namely in 'speeches with double meanings' (λόγοι ἀμφίβολοι) which can be interpreted in one way or the other and offer occasion for controversies, is said to be 'beautiful and philosophical' (καλὸν καὶ φιλόσοφον, 12.240). The striking thing is that Isocrates does not state his position either on this theory of writing with ulterior purpose or on the interpretation that his criticism of Sparta actually meant the opposite.[28]

So what did Plato think of this theory of interpretation and of 'speaking in riddles' (αἰνίττεσθαι), in which the reader has to keep hold of a secret 'covert meaning' (ὑπόνοια)?

Naturally he knows that a philosophical idea can be understood on a higher or lower level. In the *Charmides* he makes Socrates explain the concept of 'doing one's own business' (τὰ αὑτοῦ πράττειν) with intentional superficiality and perversely, not in order to refute the definition 'self-control is doing one's own business' but to establish finally that self-control cannot be 'doing one's own business' in the sense in which he has just tried to understand it; the originator of the definition expressed a 'puzzle' and did not say what he meant (*Charmides* 161c–d, 162a). But Socrates does not say in what other sense this concept might be used in any reasonable way, and we may understand this as Plato's challenge to the reader to search after that sense for himself.

On the other hand, in contrast with Isocrates' student in the *Panathenaicus*, Plato nowhere describes writing in logoi with double meanings as 'good and philosophical.' The aim of imparting knowledge is 'clarity and certainty (or stability)' of knowledge (*Phaedrus* 275c6 σαφὲς καὶ βέβαιον, 277b8–9 βεβαιότητα καὶ σαφήνειαν, cf. 278a4–5 τὸ ἐναργὲς καὶ τέλεον). This aim can only be achieved by means of the live logos of orality; but since Plato understands the written logos as an image (εἴδωλον) of the spoken one (*Phaedrus* 276a8–9), even writing must remain directed to the same aim, even if it can never achieve it (just as the replica-objects of the sensory world strive after the perfection of their original models, the Ideas, which, however, they never reach: *Phaedo* 75a–b). The view that intentional ambiguity might be able to heighten the clarity and certainty of the knowledge intended is quite definitely not Platonic. 'Covertly' imparting deeper truths about the gods in a poetic or mythological form is something which Plato rules out for the future ideal state, because the listener cannot distinguish with certainty between 'covert meaning' (ὑπόνοια) and what is asserted directly (*Republic* 2.378d). Although this is said there about the *young* recipient in particular, the problem remains the same if correspondingly more difficult 'puzzles' are placed before the advanced hearer or reader. Thus, right at the beginning of the *Republic*, Plato makes a discussion of a saying by Simonides, in which Socrates suspects a 'puzzle',[29] end with an absurd conclusion and the confusion of the interlocutor (*Republic* 1. 331d–336a). Further, we must remember Plato's heavily ironical use of the method of interpreting the names of the gods by covert interpretation and etymology in the *Cratylus* (400dff.), as well as his general dismissal of allegorical interpretations of myth in the *Phaedrus* (229c–230a), as unnecessary intellectual posing.

Plato's obvious contempt for an interpretation of the poets which is directed towards deeper meanings and his refusal to transfer this method explicitly to philosophical prose-texts or even declare himself in favour of writing in double meanings as philosophically viable make it additionally (see above, p. 31f.) quite unlikely that a corresponding literary technique could have played a central role for him.

11

THE INTERPRETATION OF SIMONIDES IN THE *PROTAGORAS*

Plato's artful and intentionally basic dramatisation of the attempt to make progress in a philosophical question by interpreting a text, which occurs in the middle section of the *Protagoras* (338e–347a), is also very important for our theme. It is shown how two extraordinarily competent interpreters, namely Protagoras and Socrates, arrive at opposite conclusions in the interpretation of the same poem.

Protagoras considers the ability to interpret literature appropriately to be the most important part of education in general (338e), so he would like to interrogate Socrates specifically on this field. He refers to a poem of Simonides which Socrates, too, as he assures Protagoras, knows very well and thinks highly of. But, in Protagoras' opinion, Simonides contradicts himself in the space of a few lines by saying first that it is difficult to become a virtuous man and then by finding fault with Pittacus for his statement that it is difficult to be noble – how can a poem be 'good' if it exhibits such a contradiction (339b–d)?

By his initial positive appraisal of the poem, Socrates is committed to 'help' the poet and thereby himself as well (βοηθεῖν τῷ ἀνδρί, 340a1; cf. 341c8–9), that is, to justify the poem and his judgment of it. Plato makes him summon up for the purpose an astoundingly advanced method of interpretation: he makes comments on the linguistic usage of Simonides, he makes use of Prodicus' synonymic approach, which was the most modern theory of semantics of the time; he more or less reconstructs the poem's intellectual horizon by identifying its hidden presuppositions; he shows that Simonides' actual intention was to correct Pittacus.

However, despite all Socrates' methodological preparation and reflectiveness, his interpretation is hardly correct in all points. In two essential points Socrates introduces his, or rather Plato's, expertise into the interpretation and thus goes substantially beyond or past Simonides' intention: first, he removes the contradiction which Protagoras sees by distinguishing between *becoming* good, which he claims is possible for a short time, and *being* good, which he says is not possible for humans for any length of time – by which Simonides, a non-metaphysical poet of the late archaic period, is saddled with Plato's ontological separation of becoming and being and, simultaneously, with Plato's conception of philosophy which says it is possible for a human being to reach the goal briefly under the stimulus of thinking, while it is impossible to stay at the goal on a lasting basis;[30] second, Socrates discovers the basic foundation of his ethics, that virtue is wisdom, foreshadowed in Simonides. In implementing both defences, a little violence to the text is necessary, and Plato himself seems to be aware of it.

It is as if Plato, by means of this first detailed literary interpretation in European intellectual history, wished to say that interpretation is necessarily misinterpretation, at least partially. Neither advanced methods nor out-of-the-ordinary intellectual ability on the part of the interpreter can alter the situation as long as the cause cannot be eliminated. But the cause consists of the fact that the interpreter necessarily imports his own point of view.

Consequently, Socrates subsequently radically devalues the whole attempt to achieve an assured interpretation of the meaning of the poem. He compares dealing with 'other people's' views with the behaviour of uneducated symposiasts who entertain themselves by means of the voice of a hired woman flute-player. Just as self-respecting symposiasts have no need of female flute-players and dancers but entertain themselves with their own contributions, so the participants assembled for the present conversation should leave the views of the poets aside and address matters directly (347c–348a). Besides, the poets cannot be asked what they are talking about and the contradictory analyses of the intended meaning are not verifiable.[31]

Thus Plato brings the interpretation of a text into sharp contrast with speaking and thinking which are one's own and which are oriented towards the objects themselves (towards the 'truth'; 348a5). This contrast between speaking with 'other people's' or with 'one's own' voice is naturally not dependent on the fact that the text which is under discussion here comes from a *poet* (and not from a philosopher). That means that for Plato *all* 'speaking with other people's voices', that is, all interpretation, is of subordinate importance. And a second failing is not peculiar only to a *poetic* text: this is the failing that the author of the text cannot be questioned in person, since he is not on the spot, and the assumptions about his meaning consequently remain uncheckable.

Both points of criticism lead away from the use of texts and towards oral philosophical inquiry which examines the matters themselves and induces the participants' own voices to speak. In a fundamental way Plato makes the contrast between the intermediary nature of all writing and the directness of oral philosophical inquiry the subject of the end of the dialogue, the *Phaedrus*.

12

THE CRITIQUE OF WRITING IN THE *PHAEDRUS*

In the final pages of the *Phaedrus* (274b–278e) Plato discusses, in a section which has become famous as the 'critique of writing', the value of writing in general and the philosopher's attitude to his writings in particular. Since the unity of thought in the *Phaedrus* is not very easy to understand, this section has all too often been treated in isolation from the overall context of the dialogue, and there has not even been any inquiry into whether there is a concrete relationship between its assertions and the structure of the other dialogues. It is, however, of decisive importance to understand the critique of writing as the culmination of the *Phaedrus*, for it is only by understanding this that the critique also becomes a key to understanding the structure of the Platonic dialogues in general.

The *Phaedrus* begins with a comparison between 'speeches' (λόγοι): the young Phaedrus reads out an elaborate speech by Lysias, whom he admires (230e–234c), and Socrates sets against it two improvised speeches (237b–241d, 243e–257b) on the same theme, namely the theme of Eros. In this comparison the main issue is not only perfection of form but from the beginning and above all the question of who has a better insight into the nature of the subject under discussion. Within the speeches the main concern is the question of who is the proper lover for a young man, the man who has fallen in love or the admirer who has not; since Socrates presents Eros in his second speech as the actual driving force of philosophy, the inquiry about the true lover turns into the inquiry about the true philosopher.

These lines of argument are initiated in the first part, but are now brought together in the critique of writing in such a way that the conditions which must be fulfilled if one speech is to be superior to the other are named in general terms, with the result that with the description of these conditions the knowledge that is necessary for the philosopher and his relations with his writings are clarified at the same time.

By 'speech', λόγος (logos), Plato means not only spoken, improvised or prepared, monological or dialogical speech but also its written 'image'. Thus he is in search of criteria which are valid for both, for what is spoken as well as what is written. But there is no room for doubt that in his opinion live, oral communication has precedence, that spoken communication is the domain by which written communication must be measured.

The quality of a logos depends on whether it is made 'in accordance with art'. A *philosophical* art of speech-making presupposes not only the mastery of the prescriptions of current rhetoric for formal structuring (these have, in reality, importance merely as preliminaries; 266d–269c), but is based on two far more ambitious and comprehensive abilities: these are the knowledge of the nature of the issues dealt with by the speech and the knowledge of the nature of the souls which the speech is meant to address (277b–c). Neither the philosophical knowledge of the issues themselves nor the knowledge of the souls addressed can be achieved either by empiricism or by the wisdom which goes with sound common sense, but only through the strenuous research of the philosophy of the Ideas which Plato defines as 'dialectic'[32] and understands as a 'long circuitous route' which can only be hinted at here in the dialogue, not embarked upon.[33]

Against the backdrop of this definition of an art of rhetoric which is 'true', i.e. based on philosophy, in the critique of writing Plato develops the particular question of the 'propriety' (εὐπρέπεια; 274b6) of the use of writing. Thus the primary issue is not the question of what writing *'can'* or *'cannot'* do; instead, this question is discussed only within the framework of the major question of how a person who wants to 'please God' (see 274b9), namely the philosopher, *should* use writing. ('Divine' is for Plato the realm of the Ideas: see e.g. *Republic* 611e2, *Phaedo* 80a3; speech and action which is 'pleasing to God' is thus the aim of the philosopher of the Ideas: *Phaedrus* 273e.)

Socrates first introduces a myth of the Egyptian god Theuth, who according to the *interpretatio Graeca* was identified with Hermes and was regarded as the discoverer of writing. The fact that Plato has recourse to the mode of mythological thought about the 'first discoverer' (the πρῶτος εὑρετής) shows that he is surveying writing in its most fundamental aspect, for in mythological thinking the inalienable nature of things was established at their original creation. So the god Theuth brought writing with other discoveries before King Thamus and praised it as a means of making the Egyptians 'wiser and stronger in memory' (σοφωτέρους καὶ μνημονικωτέρους, 274e5).

Thus Theuth represents the illusion that wisdom and insight can be won by writing, that is, 'externally, by means of signs which are foreign (to the soul)'. Theuth's illusion is utterly shattered by Thamus. Writing does not nourish but harms the memory, i.e. the soul's ability to fetch things up from within itself; it is merely a mnemonic. One does not grow wise by means of writing but is subject to the illusion that one is wise by repeated reading 'without instruction' (ἄνευ διδαχῆς, 275a7). Only διδαχή, instruction through personal intercourse, can impart clear and dependable knowledge (274e–275c).

If Plato had shared the belief of the modern theory of the dialogues (and that of Isocrates' student in the *Panathenaicus*) that despite everything writing is able to impart clear and abiding knowledge, even if only to a chosen few who are capable of understanding the subtle hints of a mode of exposition which uses double meanings, this would have been the place for Plato to have declared it. Instead, in the following pages he emphasises the basic failings of writing, which are inherent in its nature. But whatever is inherent in a thing's nature cannot be eliminated by a more or less skilful use of the thing. It is psychologically understandable that since Schleiermacher the modern devotees of the god Theuth with his faith in writing have sensed the need to reverse Plato's judgment by affirming that writing in puzzles and allusions will indeed have the desired effect of clarity and dependability of knowledge in the case of the discerning reader. However, we must assert, calmly and without any polemic, that we are here dealing with a methodologically inadmissible supplementation of the text's evidence, and indeed a supplementation which leads to the opposite of what Plato intended.

Plato arrives at the systematic delimitation of the oral from the written on the one hand by a list of the characteristics of the oral logos which are lacking from the written, and on the other hand by an impressive comparison. Let us begin with the latter.

In order to understand the comparison between the behaviour of a sensible farmer and that of a philosopher or dialectician (*Phaedrus* 276b–277a) one must know the meaning of the 'gardens of Adonis', for which our passage is the first evidence. After the end of the harvest in summer a small amount of seed was earmarked for sowing in shallow bowls or baskets, for keeping in dark conditions and for watering in such a way that the grains sprouted luxuriantly after a very short time, in the dog-days. The green bowls or baskets were then exposed to the heat of the sun, where the plants quickly wilted, naturally without having produced a yield of grain. The withered gardens of Adonis were thrown by women amidst ritual laments into the sea or springs.

The meaning of this strange custom has only recently been uncovered, by Gerhard J. Baudy. It involves an agrarian custom, a test-crop, known in other forms as well, aimed at testing the vigour of the new seed.[34] But we need not concern ourselves with this aspect of the ritual any more than with its connection with the myth of Adonis, since Plato, who presupposes the reader's knowledge of the matter, did not choose these facets of the ritual for the point of his comparison.

Instead, he argues that a sensible farmer will not seriously choose gardens of Adonis in which to sow the grains of seed from which he wants a yield, just to enjoy the beautiful growth of the plants within eight days; he will indeed do such a thing in a playful manner in honour of the Adonis-festival, but, on the strength of his knowledge of the art of agriculture, he will sow the seed about which he is serious in appropriate soil (not, that is, in clay bowls) and will be content if the seed ripens after eight months (276b). The dialectician will behave equally sensibly with his seed: he will not seriously plant it in the Adonis-gardens of writing with logoi which cannot bring support to themselves and teach the truth adequately. He will sow the gardens of writing only in play, for example when he 'tells stories' (μυθολογεῖν, 276e3; see below, p. 45f. for an explanation of the expression) about justice and related themes. What he does take seriously is the deployment of the 'art of dialectic' which he achieves by taking an 'appropriate soul' and planting logoi in it which can bring support to themselves and to the planter and not remain without yield (276c–277a).

The aspects of the ritual of the gardens of Adonis which Plato adduces for his comparison are therefore as follows:

(1) The aspect of the yield. (a) Just as there can never be a 'yield' (καρπός) of 'grains of seed' (σπέρματα)[35] in the gardens of Adonis, so, for Plato, writing is necessarily without fruit, without yield: knowledge and enthusiasm which can be communicated by writings are to be compared with the brief, illusory growth in the Adonis-garden, which is followed by a speedy wilting. (b) Because the 'yield' which the farmer aims for consists of grain (and not of the 'art

of tillage', which instead guides the activity of planting; 276b6), the 'yield' of the dialectician (λόγοι ἔχοντες σπέρμα, 277a1) must also be understood in terms of its content, i.e. consist of philosophical content (and not, for example, only of the transmission of the 'art of dialectic' as a faculty without a definite content).

(2) The aspect of duration. The little garden of Adonis grows in eight days, while serious farming takes eight months to achieve its goal. Now we can understand why the 'writing-gardens' of the dialogues always emphasise that dialectic is a 'long road' which many times exceeds the size of what is offered there in writing.[36] For Plato, the speedy process of instruction through writing which is basically insufficient (276c9) can never adequately replace oral dialectic.

(3) The aspect of choice. (a) Just as the clever farmer sows on 'suitable soil' (276b7), so the dialectician must by himself seek out a 'suitable soul' (276e6) for his philosophical sowing. Since writing can never choose its reader by itself, there is no question that it can be used for philosophical sowing 'by means of the art of dialectic' (e5). (b) There is no way that the sensible farmer will sow his entire seed-stock in Adonis-gardens: he would thereby make any yield impossible, and he would no longer qualify as a *sensible* farmer. The dialectician will likewise sow only a part of his 'grain-seed' in the gardens of writing, and he will hold back precisely those from which he hopes for a yield (276c3–9, with b2–3). At this point the comparison between the procedure of the farmer and that of the dialectician is overlaid by the contrast between 'play' and 'seriousness' so that many an interpreter has erroneously assumed that Plato is aiming at the contrast between an author who sows his *entire* seed in writing seriously, and an author who similarly sows his entire seed in writing, but only in play. Such an interpretation, however, entails neglecting the fundamental comparison: for the Greeks, planting in the Adonis-garden always meant bringing out only a part of the seed. It is only because the ritual is no longer familiar to us and because we, as children of the bookish twentieth century, have irrational prejudices against Plato's esoteric position, that we get on the wrong path of interpretation. Plato never thought of entrusting his entire philosophy to writing.

Why the dialectician exercises restraint in his dealings with writing emerges from its basic failings which Plato enumerates before the comparison:

(1) A book speaks to everyone, to people with philosophical insight, and likewise to those who have nothing to do with its contents; it cannot choose its reader, and cannot refuse to speak to

certain readers (275e2–3). For Plato, personal selection of the partner in accordance with his suitability and the possibility of also remaining silent if necessary are decisive advantages of oral philosophical inquiry (276a6–7, e6).

(2) A book always says the same thing. This is apparent when the listener or reader has a question about what is said in a book: the only 'answer' is the repetition of wording which is already known. That seems to Plato to be so far removed from real communication that he puts writing in this connection on a par with the lifeless figures of painting (275d4–9).

(3) A book cannot defend itself if it is wrongly criticised; it continuously needs the support of its author (275e3–5). The live oral logos of the person with real knowledge, i.e. the dialectician, can do precisely that – support itself. The dialectician can pass on to the 'suitable soul', i.e. the student who is amenable to philosophy, the ability to support the logos and its creator (276e5–277a3).

Here as well we must repeat categorically what we observed in connection with the section on Theuth (above, p. 40f.): if, in the spirit of modern theory about the dialogues, Plato had believed that the written logos of the dialogues in fact does not speak to everyone inasmuch as it knows how to address suitable people in a specifically directed manner, and that the logos does not merely repeat itself, inasmuch as it gives different answers to different readers in accordance with their stage of development, and that the logos does indeed in some way know how to support itself, this would have been the place to state it unequivocally. As things stand, however, there is no suggestion whatsoever that any type of the use of writing, whether one which is already known of or one which still lies in the future,[37] could ever adequately perform the tasks of the oral logos. Indeed, we do not need to conclude from this that Plato did not know of 'indirect communication' by means of intimations and allusions which the reader himself must supply with meaning;[38] but it does follow that 'indirect communication' cannot have played the decisive role in his view of the function and value of writing which Schleiermacher and his countless successors in the nineteenth and twentieth centuries have ascribed to it. It is also easy to see why this could not have been the case: the art of the allusive 'speeches with double meanings' (λόγοι ἀμφίβολοι) can perform the tasks of an oral speech only in a metaphorical sense, as I shall explain in greater detail below (p. 109f.). But choice of partner, silence when confronted with unsuitable people, supporting by new arguments, are not metaphors in Plato's way of thinking, but have to be understood as the basic conditions for the philosophical communication of knowledge.

Since written logoi cannot produce the effects we have been discussing, the value of the best of them is limited in Plato's thinking to that of *aides-mémoire* for the person who possesses knowledge (εἰδότων ὑπόμνησιν 278a1; cf. ὑπομνήματα θησαυριζόμενος 276d3). Writing can indeed be an *aide-mémoire* in many ways, and unfortunately Plato does not specify which particular way he had in mind. Thus it has recently been suggested that the aporetic dialogues be understood as such *aides-mémoire*: in that case, Plato's students in the Academy would be the 'people who possess knowledge', who on the basis of certain prior knowledge were able to solve the problems which the aporetic dialogues presented.[39] It is possible that Plato had such a thing in mind too. But one must remember that the constructive dialogues, which are more likely to be regarded as Plato's 'best writings', cannot be *aides-mémoire*, in any case not in this sense. Moreover, it is doubtful whether Plato would have classed students who must be tested by means of such exercises as 'people who possess knowledge' (in the other passages of the *Phaedrus* the expression unequivocally means the dialectician). Indeed, it might even be asked whether a student who for example knew the doctrine of anamnesis in the form in which it exists in the *Meno* really needed the aporias of the *Euthydemus* as an exercise.

However that may be, at 276d3 Plato mentions that the philosopher sets up *aides-mémoire* not only for people of like mind but also for himself, for the time when he reaches forgetful old age. The aporetic dialogues can certainly be eliminated for this purpose. The emphasis laid on the function of reminding makes us moderns think perhaps primarily of works like the *Timaeus* and the *Laws*, which are rich respectively in scientific or juridical and historical details. We cannot tell for sure to what extent 'hypomnematic' writings in the narrower sense were also intended – for example, collections of details related to the most varied fields of knowledge, including the genre of 'Divisions' and 'Definitions'.[40]

However, let us not forget that setting up *aides-mémoire* is not the only reason for the writings of the philosopher to exist – Plato also mentions the 'game' whose success gives pleasure to the author (276d4–8). There is no reason not to apply this word to Plato personally, especially since shortly after this he weaves in a pretty clear allusion to his own 'mythical', i.e. story-telling, 'game' with the concept of justice in the *Republic*.[41] Plato found the charming and entertaining dramatisation of philosophical conversations a witty game which gave him great pleasure. The dialogues owe their existence not least to this brilliant writer's artistic instinct for play.

13

THE DEFINITION OF THE PHILOSOPHER BASED ON HIS RELATIONSHIP TO HIS WRITINGS

Plato's considerations on the relative value of oral and written logoi lead up to a message which Socrates gives to Phaedrus for him to deliver to Lysias – but apart from Lysias the message is directed to Homer and Solon as well. None of the three names stands for individuals but representatively for whole areas of literature: Homer for the whole of poetry (278c2–3), Lysias for non-philosophical prose, Solon for philosophy, especially for ethical and legislatory philosophy. At the same time, the three names stand for three epochs of Greek intellectual history and without doubt are meant to represent the entirety of the Greeks' literary tradition symbolically. Thus Socrates says to Phaedrus to go and tell this entire tradition that, if an author composed his works

> knowing the facts about truth, and capable of supporting [them] if he engages in an analytical discussion about what he has written, and capable of proving what he has written to be trivial (φαῦλα) by means of his oral opinion ['by speaking himself', λέγων αὐτός], such an author must not be described by a term taken from these [sc. his works], but from what he directs his serious attention to.

Phaedrus: So what kind of names would you assign to him?
Socrates: Calling him 'wise', Phaedrus, seems to me to be going a little too far, and to be appropriate only to a god; but 'friend of wisdom' (φιλόσοφος) or something of that kind might be more fitting and also be more proper for him.

Phaedrus: And quite appropriate.

Socrates: On the other hand, anyone who does not have anything more valuable (τὸν μὴ ἔχοντα τιμιώτερα) than what he has composed and written, turning it over this way and that for a long time, sticking things together and taking them apart, you would, presumably rightly, address as 'poet' or 'speech-writer' or 'law-writer'?

Phaedrus: What else? (*Phaedrus* 278c4–e3).

Here Plato separates all authors into two very unequal groups. The one group, undoubtedly the majority, can be called poets, speech-writers or law-writers in accordance with their respective literary productions. The other group receives a name which not only separates them from God but also associates them with him – for only in the name of the *philosophos* is there an echo of the distinguishing quality of God, being wise (*sophos*). The *philosophos* owes his greater nearness to God to his 'knowing': the person 'who knows the facts about truth' (who is εἰδὼς ᾗ τὸ ἀληθὲς ἔχει, 278c4–5) is no other than the dialectician who possesses knowledge of the Just, Beautiful and Good (276c3) and who makes use of the art of dialectic, in other words the thinker who recognises the truth of things in accordance with the doctrine of the Ideas (cf. also 277b, as well as 273d–274a).

It is to this knowledge of the Ideas that the *philosophos* owes a superiority over his writings which distinguishes him alone: he is in the position to support his writings whenever he embarks upon the process of examination and 'refutation' (ἔλεγχος), and can at the same time prove through oral demonstration that what he has written is trivial (δυνατὸς τὰ γεγραμμένα φαῦλα ἀποδεῖξαι, 278c6–7). Anyone 'who possesses nothing more worthwhile than what he has composed or written, turning it over this way and that over a long period of time, sticking things together and taking them apart' (278d8–e1) belongs to the other group of non-philosophical authors.

The philosopher can thus support his writings orally, through better argumentation – how else could he prove his writings to be of negligible value? Something which is correct in terms of its content can for all that be 'badly' said (φαύλως) – namely at the moment when adequate substantiation is lacking (see *Republic* 449c4–8). Plato now defines these better arguments as 'more valuable' by summarising with the expression τὸν μὴ ἔχοντα τιμιώτερα (278d8) what the non-philosopher lacks: knowledge of the Ideas, and as a consequence the ability to 'support' and to show up the lesser value of what is written. From this negative expression, which forms the antithesis to 'the person with knowledge' (278c4), we can conclude that for Plato ἔχειν τιμιώτερα, that is, the possession of something of greater value than his writings, is a positive characteristic of the dialectician.

Defining the philosopher in the light of his relationship to his writings has implications which we must think through.

One possibility is that an author only sometimes has at his disposal 'things which are more valuable' than his writings, but sometimes he does not. Then he will sometimes be able to 'support' his writings and prove them trivial, but, once again, sometimes he will not. Consequently, sometimes he will deserve the name *philosophos*, sometimes he will not. But it tells against this possibility that the difference between the philosopher and the non-philosopher is an absolutely fundamental one for Plato. Becoming a philosopher entails experiencing a 'turning of the soul' (ψυχῆς περιαγωγή, *Republic* 521c6; cf. 518d4) which alters one's whole life. What marks out the philosopher is a completely altered attitude to reality – only he is capable of a knowledge of the Ideas. Everywhere that Plato adduces the concept of the *philosophos* he refers to this ontological reorientation (see *Phaedo* 101e, *Symposium* 204bff. [Eros as *philosophos*], *Republic* 474bff., *Phaedrus* 249c, *Theaetetus* 172c–177c, *Timaeus* 53d). Thus nothing is more improbable than that Plato could, here in the critique of writing, make the name *philosophos* dependent on a changing disposition.[42] In fact, nothing in the text suggests that an author who is worthy of the name *philosophos* today could be relegated to the category of the poets or speech-writers tomorrow.

Thus it follows that the *philosophos* in Plato's sense *always* has *timiôtera* at his disposal. Here again two possibilities present themselves: the one is that he has set down everything that he has to say, and can advance unlimitedly with further arguments. But in that case the upshot would be that for Plato argumentation was an infinite regress which never reaches an end. As is well known, however, the contrary view lies at the basis of the Platonic conception of philosophy: dialectic leads to an ἀνυπόθετον, to a non-hypothetical principle of everything, or, to put it in other words, there is an 'end of the journey' (τέλος τῆς πορείας, *Republic* 532e3) for the dialectician. And something else tells against the possibility: the dialectician would not be behaving like the clever farmer who would never sow his entire seed in his Adonis-gardens.

The only remaining possibility is the one which the comparison with the farmer (276b–c) was working up to, along with the emphasis placed on the ability to remain silent if necessary (276a7). Only if we accept that Plato's author must indeed behave like the sensible farmer can we interpret the definition of the philosopher in the critique of writing in a way which is free of contradiction: only if the philosopher consciously keeps his last arguments out of the Adonis-gardens of writing can we be sure that he really is in the position to leave his own writings behind him through 'more valuable things'; it is only on this condition that we can dismiss the definitely unPlatonic view that the quality of being a philosopher will one moment be ascribed to an author and the next moment be denied him according to the uncertain success of support which he improvises *ad hoc*; and it is only on this condition that support which is always available will not have to end in an unPlatonic *regressus in infinitum*.

14

THE MEANING OF
ΤΙΜΙΩΤΕΡΑ

In our interpretation of the critique of writing we applied the word τιμιώτερα (*timiôtera*) to philosophical *subject-matter*: by the 'more valuable things' Plato means concepts and theories, propositions and arguments in their favour to which a greater philosophical importance can be attached in comparison with other propositions and arguments. Since the expression *timiôtera* has, however, often been misunderstood (see below, p. 53f.) we would do well to define its meaning directly from its context in the *Phaedrus* and related passages in Plato.

In the critique of writing the point is that the philosopher's spoken logos must as a general principle be able to surpass his own written logos by coming to its support with better conceptual tools. But surpassing one logos by another is a theme which is already dealt with – as we saw briefly above, p. 39f. – in the first part of the dialogue: after Phaedrus reads out a speech of Lysias which is set in writing (230e–234c), in the course of conversation with Socrates it is made clear how one speech must be constituted if it is to surpass the one which is offered first (234e–236b). The new speech must offer *more* in terms of its content, and not merely quantitatively but also in terms of its philosophical importance: what is required is not merely 'more' but 'additional' and 'better' subject-matter, of 'higher value'.[43] Thus the reader knows from the beginning what conditions a superior logos must fulfil. Indeed, Socrates' speeches about Eros entirely fulfil these conditions. Thus the critique of writing basically only expresses in a general form what Plato demonstrates in the course of the dialogue. Accordingly, the interpretation which chooses not to understand the *timiôtera* on the basis of philosophical content breaks an important connection of thought which is clearly marked out by Plato himself. Moreover, in order not to let any obscurity arise, Plato continues this connection beyond the critique

51

of writing through to the epilogue of the *Phaedrus*: there, in an obvious prediction based on hindsight, it is said of Isocrates (who like Lysias composed court-speeches for others, but then changed his profession and became a respected teacher of rhetoric and the author of writings on politics and educational theory) that he would surpass Lysias and devote himself to 'greater things' (279a8). This expression too is immediately understandable as yet another synonym for the 'more valuable things'.[44] In the whole dialogue we are thus always dealing with the same thought: the philosophical ranking of the content of a logos decides the ranking of the logos. Consequently, the fact that *timiôtera* appear in the spoken support of the philosopher means that he will explain more important things by the spoken word than in writing.

A meaning other than one relating to content was not at all to be expected of Plato's linguistic usage. The 'most important and highest-ranking (most valuable) things' (τὰ μέγιστα καὶ τιμιώτατα) are, according to the *Politicus* (285e4), the incorporeal entities of the world of the Ideas; in the *Phaedrus* the Ideas are likewise in their entirety τίμια, i.e. 'of (high) ranking or value' (250b2). At one point in the *Republic* a distinction is drawn between high-ranking and low-ranking 'parts' (τιμιώτερον/ἀτιμότερον μέρος, 485b6) within the world of the Ideas.

For Plato the ultimate source of 'ranking' and 'value' is the Idea of the Good itself[45] as the principle of everything. But knowledge participates in the rank of the Good too,[46] naturally to the extent that it directs itself to the origin. But the logoi which express knowledge partake in its ranking, for they are, according to *Timaeus* 29b, related to the thing which they deal with. In general, knowledge is of higher ranking than right opinion (τιμιώτερον ἐπιστήμη ὀρθῆς δόξης, *Meno* 98a7) because it 'binds fast' with arguments what is correct about the opinion. The final substantiation must come from the 'principle of everything' (from the ἀρχὴ πάντων); the ascent to the principle is by steps, from hypothesis to 'higher (ἄνωθεν) hypothesis' right to the 'non-hypothetical' (ἀνυπόθετον; see *Phaedo* 101d–e, *Republic* 511b). For its part, the generally 'high-ranking' or 'valuable' argument must grow step by step in its ranking, when it succeeds in connecting the insights gained to concepts which are closer to the principle, closer in the sense of 'the things which are linked with the principle' (*Republic* 511b8). 'Possessing something of greater value' (ἔχειν τιμιώτερα) thus means for the dialectician the same as being in the position to substantiate an explanation he has given in such a way that the process of 'binding fast' by means of arguments takes a starting-point which is 'higher' in the scale of hypotheses.

Another result of what has been said is that the 'more valuable' or 'higher-ranking' logos must also be the more scientific, the more strict one. It is clear from this why the dialectician sees his 'serious activity' in his oral philosophical inquiry and his 'play' in writing for a necessarily mixed and scientifically untutored audience. In comparison with the spoken word, the written word is φαῦλον (*Phaedrus* 278c7), which is to be understood here in the well-attested meaning of 'unspecialised, untechnical'.

We should note in passing that the use of *timion* by Aristotle and Theophrastus suggests that the word became a technical term in the Early Academy for describing the ontological status of the first principle (ἀρχή, *archê*).[47] The Platonic idea that the status of knowledge is determined by the status of its object, an idea which, as is well known, forms the basis of the doctrine of the Ideas (see *Republic* 474b–480a), is preserved by Aristotle, as is shown for example by the beginning of the *De Anima*:[48]

> If we proceed from the assumption that knowledge belongs to noble and valuable things (τῶν καλῶν καὶ τιμίων), and one form of knowledge more than the other, either on the basis of its exactness or because it addresses better and more impressive objects (τῷ βελτιόνων τε καὶ θαυμασιωτέρων εἶναι), we shall on both counts with good reason consider studying the soul as one of the most important forms of knowledge.
>
> (402a1–4)

The upshot of all this is that no member of the Early Academy or the Peripatos would have had any doubt that the Platonic 'things of higher value' (τιμιώτερα) are to be related to philosophical subject-matter and that they owe their status to the way the arguments for them are traced back to the *archê*, the source of all status and value.

A common misunderstanding of the 'more valuable things' arises from not recognising the overarching connections within the *Phaedrus*, ignoring Plato's linguistic usage and then, with the horizon thus narrowed, attempting to deny the reference to philosophical subject-matter by stating that what is meant is the activity of spoken discussion which of itself should be preferred to writing. The real motive behind denying the obviously correct interpretation in terms of subject-matter is of course the anti-esoteric prejudice of the twentieth century: it is not willingly admitted that the Platonic dialectician could intentionally leave fundamental subject-matter aside. (The same interpreters then do not wish either to admit that in the *Phaedrus* there are two clear references to leaving important areas blank: 246a and 274a.)

Let us briefly consider the consequences which would result if this interpretation were correct. If it is irrelevant to require arguments of greater meaning in terms of subject-matter, the philosopher's oral defence of the written word would end up the way we are familiar with from every possible field and from our everyday experience, namely continuing to speak in a soothing and conciliatory manner on the same level of reflectiveness as writing itself, which is to be 'supported'. However, such support will as usual be more concerned with proving one's own writings to be correct and valid, while Plato's dialectician will prove his writing as nothing less than 'of negligible value' by the support which he brings it orally. Furthermore, any more or less intelligent author is capable of giving the usual support without arguments of higher standard in terms of subject-matter; but that would mean that anybody who is not completely lacking in talent would be worthy of the name of *philosophos*, even if he had never studied the Platonic dialectic of the Ideas. Indeed there have been recent commentators who have believed that Plato is 'offering' this title to all sorts of authors inasmuch as they put on only a 'qualified attitude' towards their own writing. But we have already seen that the 'man with knowledge' who is the subject of the critique of writing (276a8, c3–4, 278a1, c4) can only be the man who knows the Platonic philosophy of the Ideas and dialectic (see 276e5–6, 277b5–8). And in view of the importance which the designation *philosophos* had for Plato (see above, p. 47f.), we can have little faith in a solution which can consider it conceivable that this title should all of a sudden be easy for anyone to have. Moreover, this solution was formulated in obvious ignorance of the fact that the dialogues show clearly enough in numerous passages how the spoken 'support' of the dialectician proceeds, and in ignorance of the fact that they thereby fully and completely confirm the interpretation of the 'things of greater value' in terms of subject-matter.

15

'SUPPORT FOR THE LOGOS' IN
THE DIALOGUES

Since the dialogues are 'images' of the live speech of the man with
knowledge (see *Phaedrus* 276a), they can also give an image of the
characteristic *oral* procedure of the dialectician, namely the 'support'
he gives to his logos. It might at first sight appear a contradiction
that oral support is represented in written works. But there would
only be a contradiction if a written dialogue claimed to contain the
'support' which it stands in need of itself. But, as is well known, the
opposite is the case: in the 'gaps' the dialogues refer to theories
which are not imparted on the spot but which would be necessary
for their own substantiation, or 'support' them. The fact that in
Platonic dialogues one written logos supports another which is
likewise written is in itself free of contradiction and totally
unproblematical, provided that the reader knows unambiguously
that the dialogue bringing support, as a written dialogue, naturally also needs support which it cannot give itself. To put it
another way, it is only the higher stages of support leading to the
recognition of the fundamental principle (the *archê*) which Plato
could not have entrusted to writing without self-contradiction.
But the Platonic dialogues quite obviously do not contravene this
condition.

The situation involving βοήθεια, that is, the situation in which
a logos is exposed to an attack and its author is required to support
it, is the central structural principle of the Platonic dialogues. There
are cases where the word 'supporting' (βοηθεῖν) is used explicitly,
and others where it is replaced by a synonymous expression, but the
basic situation always remains the same. The question is always the
same, namely whether the author of the logos is capable of bringing
support by means of new and more weighty modes of thought and
arguments, i.e. with *timiôtera*; if he can, he is the *philosophos*. The
discussion-leader, who represents the figure of the dialectician,

always stands the test when confronted with this task: everyone else fails, for only the man capable of contemplating the Ideas is indeed a *philosophos*. Let us now turn to the evidence.[49]

(a) Three examples of Platonic 'support'

(1) In the *Phaedo*, immediately after Simmias' and Cebes' objections to the immortality of the soul (84c–88b), there follows an interruption in the narrated dialogue. In Plato's works this procedure always has the function of providing what follows with a strong emphasis. The listener of the framing dialogue, Echecrates, wishes to know from Phaedo, the narrator, how Socrates reacted to the crisis in the discussion which the Theban friends triggered, whether he was angry or 'did he calmly try to support his logos? And did he support it adequately or unsatisfactorily?' (πράως ἐβοήθει τῷ λόγῳ; καὶ ἱκανῶς ἐβοήθησεν ἢ ἐνδεῶς, 88d9–e3). Thus Echecrates asks how Socrates reacted in human terms and in terms of his arguments. Phaedo then goes on to report how admirably Socrates acquitted himself in both respects. His βοηθεῖν τῷ λόγῳ was capable of satisfying his critics, a fact which is commented on incidentally in a second interruption of the narrative of the dialogue, which of course is designed to add emphasis to the first one (102a). In order to refute the objection of Cebes, Socrates temporarily leaves the theme of the 'soul' (from 96a) in order to propose a comprehensive theory of the cause of coming into existence and passing out of it ('for we must in general terms examine the cause of coming into existence and passing out of it', ὅλως γὰρ δεῖ περὶ γενέσεως καὶ φθορᾶς τὴν αἰτίαν διαπραγματεύεσθαι, 95e9–96a1); this theory leads, as we know, to the exposition of the hypothesis of the Ideas (99dff.), on the basis of which the problem of the soul can be discussed as a subordinate special case, so to speak (105bff.).

We may summarise the characteristics of this section of the discussion as follows:

1 The person who carries out the successful βοηθεῖν τῷ λόγῳ is the discussion-leader (naturally not Simmias or Cebes).
2 In order to help his first logos (on the soul), Socrates first talks about other matters (the Ideas etc.). He temporarily changes the theme (without in the meantime losing sight of the general theme of 'immortality').
3 This additional theme relates to a theory of greater scope which leads closer to a knowledge of the first causes. Proceeding by

hypotheses involves a successive ascent to a ἱκανόν which is obviously to be viewed as the *archê* (101d–e; cf. 107b). In that the supporting logos opens the way to knowledge which is more comprehensive and better based, it is, in terms of the facts, justified to talk of a theory which is 'of higher value'.

(2) At the beginning of the second book of the *Republic* we hear an attack by Glaucon and Adeimantus on justice, which Socrates had successfully defended against Thrasymachus in the first book. Socrates is challenged to support justice (and therefore naturally support his first logos in favour of justice), and he himself recognises this as his duty. The expression βοηθεῖν appears no less than five times in this connection.[50] The 'support' which Socrates brings justice encompasses the whole line of argumentation right up to Book 10. In order to acquire a theory of justice, he changes the immediate subject of discussion and talks about the best state and about the soul; in order to defend his concept of the state further, he talks about the difference between Idea and particular, about the nature and the education of the philosopher, and, within the framework of the last theme, about the 'greatest object of instruction' (μέγιστον μάθημα) of all, the Idea of the Good, which is the 'principle of all things'. 'Supporting' justice is therefore a scaled ascent,[51] if not right to the knowledge of the *archê* (whose τί ἐστιν is left out of consideration, 506d–e), then into its immediate vicinity. The Good itself is in absolute terms the thing of highest value (ἔτι μειζόνως τιμητέον τὴν τοῦ ἀγαθοῦ ἕξιν, 509a4–5; cf. b9), so that explanations which are aimed at it are correctly to be described as *timiôtera* in comparison with theories and arguments which aim at anything less.

(3) The support which the Athenian brings the law of impiety in the *Laws* bears great similarity to the support which Socrates brings justice in the *Republic*. The almost identical reference to a duty to support,[52] understood in religious terms, by itself demonstrates sufficiently that the two operations have the same intention. The Athenian is anticipating an attack by atheists on the law he has just formulated. This law will, like all laws, be promulgated in writing to the citizens of the new Cretan state that is to be founded (891a); however, even in this oral conversation with Clinias and Megillus, the author has the arguments ready by which writing will have to be defended at that juncture. What is meant is not a juridical and political defence, which of course every lawgiver should have ready, no matter how untrained he might be as a philosopher. Rather,

the discussion-leader hesitates to begin with the ἐπαμύνοντες λόγοι,[53] for these would make it an unavoidable necessity to 'step outside the lawgiving process' (νομοθεσίας ἐκτὸς βαίνειν, 891d7). In the course of his help the Athenian does indeed abandon the usual level and the topic up to this point and discusses, in order to secure the foundations for the law against impiety, the concept of movement, the self-movement of the soul, the priority of the soul over the body, the role of the Good and the Bad in the cosmos, and the direction of the universe by the gods (891b–899c). Thus the *Laws* (like the *Republic*) upholds all the characteristic qualities of support as we defined them in the case of the *Phaedo*. Furthermore, this text demonstrates with exemplary clarity that one cannot attain to Platonic support 'in any other way' (μηδαμῇ ἑτέρως) than by means of ἐκτὸς βαίνειν, that is, through changing the topic (891d7–e1), and that this procedure leads closer to the πρῶτα τῶν πάντων (891c2–3, with e5–6).

Thus Platonic 'support' (βοήθεια) is the method of the discussion-leader (the representative of the 'dialectician'-type) for defending his logos when it has come under attack, by leaving the theme behind for the moment and advancing on the path to knowing the *archai* in order to present a sound foundation for his original logos by means of theories of 'higher standing'.

(b) The unchanging situations where βοήθεια occurs

Apart from βοηθεῖν (αὐτῷ or τῷ λόγῳ or τοῖς λόγοις), we hear of ἀμύνειν/ἀμύνεσθαι (cf. ἐπαμύνοντες λόγοι) and ἐπικουρεῖν or ἐπίκουρον γίγνεσθαι as Plato's expressions of supporting. Plato's well-known distaste for fixed terminologies[54] makes it no surprise that he varied this key-term of his criticism of writing further. In order to discover synonyms one must start from the basic and unchanging *situations*: a logos is formulated ('the soul is immortal'; 'justice is better than injustice'), initial arguments are proposed – but the πατὴρ τοῦ λόγου undergoes the elenchus, i.e. he is challenged to show that he is a *philosophos*, by tracing his logos back to deeper fundamentals.

It is important that, according to the evidence of *Phaedrus* 278c–d, *both the philosopher and the non-philosopher* are to be measured against this kind of elenchus. It is therefore only to be expected that in the dialogues quite different types of human beings are subjected to the elenchus, but only one type, the philosopher, passes its test. It is of importance, furthermore, that the dialectician can impart the capacity to support (*Phaedrus* 276ef.); precisely for that reason we shall recognise the teacher who cannot do that as a non-philosopher.

This is the case with Gorgias, whose pupil Polus would like to 'reconstruct' the logos of his teacher after Socrates' criticisms (*Gorgias* 462a2). He fails, like Callicles after him, because his teacher is not a *philosophos* in Plato's sense, and consequently was not able to teach how to ἐπανορθώσασθαι τὸν λόγον (= βοηθεῖν τῷ λόγῳ).[55]

The situation in the *Hippias Maior* is rather less obvious because it is overlaid by gross irony. Socrates wants to make Hippias into the superior teacher from whom he would like to learn in order to 'fight his way through the conversation again' (286d7 ἀναμαχούμενος τὸν λόγον) after his alleged defeat in discussion with an anonymous third person. What Hippias offers as a means for resuming the conversation is indeed (ironically) assessed by Socrates as his support (ὅτι μοι δοκεῖς ... βοηθεῖν, 291e5). In reality the anonymous third person is only a transparent mask for the inner voice of Socrates (see esp. 304d), who is thus the person who remains victorious in this conversation as well, not least because of the way he reaches for more comprehensive themes in the excursus after Hippias' attack (300b ff.).

Sharpest irony is what also typifies the shorter conversation with Hippias. In a 'fit' (καταβολή, *Hippias Minor* 372e1) Socrates upholds a morally indefensible proposition from which he would like Hippias to 'heal' him. The request 'Don't refuse to heal my soul' (μὴ φθονήσῃς ἰάσασθαι τὴν ψυχήν μου, 372e6–7) means in the context of the situation in the dialogue nothing other than 'support your logos' (βοήθησον τῷ σαυτοῦ λόγῳ), for Hippias has represented the ethically correct view – if he could only substantiate it more deeply he might be able to heal Socrates' 'fit'; but Hippias is not a *philosophos* and the 'healing-process', like all his other attempts to support his logos, fails to eventuate.

The ironical elevation of the opponent is driven to extremes in the *Euthydemus*. Both students of eristics are called on for help 'like the Dioscuri' (293a2). Their beneficial intervention would be indeed comparable with the 'healing of the soul' expected of Hippias. Since Socrates has sarcastically raised his opponents to the level of the helpers-in-need Castor and Polydeuces, he does not talk in terms of 'support' anymore but of 'rescue' from the start: δεόμενος τοῖν ξένοιν ... σῶσαι ἡμᾶς ... ἐκ τῆς τρικυμίας τοῦ λόγου (293a1–3; ~ δεόμενος βοηθῆσαι τῷ λόγῳ ἡμῶν).[56] The students of eristics are thus asked to support someone else's logos: that too is part of the skill of a dialectician (to the extent that the logos in need of support allows it), as the dialogues *Cratylus* and *Theaetetus* show. Here Socrates defends Cratylus' position up to a point (Cratylus himself is present) or that of Protagoras (who is represented by his pupil Theodorus); but, characteristically, he himself must take over the task of supporting for the others, and in the last analysis this does not lead very far: only the position based on the philosophy of the Ideas can stand up to every elenchus. In Plato's sense, supporting is not a question of intellectual versatility but of the correct ontological point of view.

The idea, turned into comedy in the *Hippias Maior*, that Socrates when defeated in conversation seeks philosophical instruction from a person who is 'more wise' is something which Plato formulates again, and this time without any comic intention, in the *Symposium*. Socrates, who allegedly labours under the same illusions as Agathon (*Symposium* 201e), questioned the wise Diotima, in order to learn something about Eros. This time his expectations did not deceive him. But the prophetess of Mantinea, Diotima, is as much a fictitious character as the anonymous third person in the *Hippias Maior*. It is therefore again Socrates who continues the discussion. And it is obvious how he reaches far beyond the framework of his conversation with Agathon about Eros in the speech he attributes to Diotima and deals with things of greater philosophical importance which lead closer to a knowledge of the *archê*.

So much for parallel situations and synonyms. It should have become clear that the concept of βοηθεῖν τῷ λόγῳ characterises the structural principle of the Platonic dialogue; it consists of intentionally elevating the level of argumentation towards an ultimate argument based on the *archê*.

16

THE ASCENT TO THE PRINCIPLES AND THE LIMITS OF PHILOSOPHICAL COMMUNICATION

Plato states more than once that the aim of the man of knowledge is to ascend to a final, transcendental principle. He may talk about an ascent from hypothesis to hypothesis to reach something which is 'sufficient' (ἱκανόν, *Phaedo* 99d–107b), or about an ascending recognition of the Beautiful from observing beautiful bodies, past the recognition of the morally beautiful up to the contemplation of the Beautiful itself (*Symposium* 210aff.), or about the gradation of the modes of perception, the highest of which, νόησις, recognises the principle of all things (*Republic* 509d–511e).[57] At any rate the meaning of these passages has not been misunderstood by previous generations, who regarded the desire for 'ascent' and 'climbing over' as the essence of Platonism.

But it has been recognised much less often that ascent is the actual theme of the dialogues' dramatic representation. Whenever scholars have noticed this,[58] their emphasis has been on the ascent as such, and it has been forgotten that the dialogues always illustrate only one section of the ascent and make the intentional limitations of the process perfectly clear. It is only when we understand the critique of writing correctly that we can understand why the two things hang together – the ascent and the limitations of its presentation in writing, 'supporting' through 'more valuable things' and 'remaining silent' when it is necessary (σιγᾶν πρὸς οὓς δεῖ). The examples adduced above for Platonic 'support' (pp. 55–58) are examples not only of resorting to *timiôtera* but also of clear cases of 'gaps'.

It is significant that Plato's *timiôtera* point in the final analysis to the recognition of the prime principles in view of the fact that

Aristotle in his *Metaphysics* and other works refers to a doctrine of principles not found in this form in the dialogues. This discrepancy has led to a quite unnecessary confusion in Platonic studies. The vast majority of scholars has not been ready to accept that Aristotle, who spent twenty years in Plato's Academy, could know more precise details of Plato's doctrine of principles than is possible for the modern student of Plato as long as he sticks to the dialogues alone. In consequence, the attempt has been made to play down Aristotle's statements: some scholars have wanted to limit the doctrine of principles, which grew more and more evident in outline, to a particular phase in Plato's life, namely to his very last years – the old Plato, they say, simply did not have the time to write yet another dialogue on the subject; others have thought that they could understand the Aristotelian statements as mere interpretations. The Platonic scholars' abiding incapability to recognise a real Platonic doctrine of prime principles was caused among other things by the fact that no one had a clear concept of the possible reasons why Plato might reserve opinion in writing.

Why must it be precisely the section of Plato's philosophy that deals with prime principles which has to be defended against written dissemination? Against the background of the critique of writing the answer is simple: the more complex the subject, the greater the probability that uncomprehending people will unjustifiably dismiss it, a situation which the author cannot ward off in his absence (see *Phaedrus* 275d–e). Plato clearly did not think such dismissal a matter of indifference – which is perfectly comprehensible if one considers that for him the world of the Ideas had a 'divine' status 'beyond the heavens'.[59] It is perhaps more important that Plato thought it meaningless to pass on to anyone things for which he is not suited, or not yet sufficiently trained. He calls such things ἀπρόρρητα (*aprorrhêta*) – 'things which must not be passed on prematurely', because, if they are passed on prematurely, i.e. before the recipient is ready for them, they 'explain nothing' (*Laws* 968e4–5). Since the theory of principles is the area of philosophy which generally makes the greatest demands, any adequate preparation for it by means of writing, which is, however, 'incapable of teaching the truth adequately' (*Phaedrus* 276c9), is ruled out, and as a consequence even fixing it in writing would also be only counterproductive.

Instead of extracting these simple but fundamental insights from the dialogues and applying them to the dialogues themselves, scholars have shied away from the idea that a 'secret doctrine' might be ascribed to Plato[60] and have thought that they would be able to exonerate him from that charge only by denying him a theory of principles. Other scholars have constructed the unnecessary objection that, if we accept an unwritten theory of principles, we must also accept that Plato had two distinct spheres for his philosophy, one for written philosophical inquiry, another for oral.[61] The objection misunderstands the relationship of orality and literacy in Plato; we are not dealing with two distinct spheres of subject-matter but with a continuing philosophical inquiry into the same problems, raising the level of argumentation step by step.

Both attempts to get rid of Aristotle's evidence on Plato's 'unwritten teachings' are doomed to failure. There is neither any means of showing that these statements are mere interpretations[62] (on the contrary, for here as elsewhere Aristotle distinguishes very clearly between what his opponents said and what he thinks follows from their hypotheses),[63] nor is it acceptable to narrow the doctrine of principles down chronologically to Plato's later period. It is not only in the *Republic* that the education of the philosopher-kings culminates in the dialectic understanding of the Idea of the Good as the *archê* of everything (504aff., 532eff., 540a); the relatively early dialogues the *Charmides* and the *Lysis* display the idea of the ascent which cannot be broken off until a first principle, an *archê*, has been reached: if we want to explore φιλία we must go back to a 'first dear thing', a πρῶτον φίλον (*Lysis* 219c–d); if we wish to understand self-restraint, the 'knowledge of the Good and the Bad' appears on the horizon of the discussion (*Charmides* 174b–c).[64] It is precisely in this dialogue on self-restraint in the *Charmides* that, as was mentioned briefly above, p. 15f., we find a transparent metaphorical usage of the concepts of 'medical remedy' (φάρμακον, *pharmakon*) and 'incantation' (ἐπῳδή, *epôdê*) which can make us understand Plato's attitude to writing about the *archai*: Socrates claims to have a *pharmakon* for the illness of the young Charmides: but the *pharmakon* is not handed over on the grounds that it is effective only with an incantation, and useless without it (155e8) and because Socrates had given an oath to the Thracian priest who had given him the incantation and the *pharmakon* never to allow himself to be persuaded to hand on the *pharmakon* without the incantation of the recipient's soul (157b1–c6). There can be no doubt that the imagery of the *pharmakon* carries a statement about the correct manner of communicating philosophical knowledge.[65] Plato gives us to understand that Socrates as the dialectician has insights at his disposal which would indeed be directly communicable, but which he deliberately does not communicate because they would be useless for Charmides as long as he has not obtained the correct preparation for understanding the 'remedy' in the form of preliminary 'incantations'. The *pharmakon* thus stands for central principles of dialectic knowledge of the Good and the Bad; these principles can be formulated (there is no question here whatsoever about the inexpressible in philosophy), and they could consequently be formulated and disseminated in writing as well. What stops Socrates from passing on the *pharmakon* is an oath which he had given his Thracian teacher – thus the dialectician also has the responsibility, which he feels just as strongly as a sworn religious obligation, to hand down his 'things of greater value' only when the cognitive and ethical conditions are present which will ensure that they will be received appropriately. But, as we know full well, writing can never produce these conditions.

What the early *Charmides* tells us by means of metaphors is explicitly expressed by the late *Timaeus*, namely that it is the principles in particular which cannot be communicated to everyone. The mythical figure of the Demiurge is doubtless the name for a principle of the world-order within the framework of the *Timaeus*. It is difficult, Plato says, to find this creator and father of the cosmos, but to communicate him to everyone once he has been found is impossible (*Timaeus* 28c3–5). According to another passage it is the 'even higher principles' (αἱ δ᾿ ἔτι τούτων ἀρχαὶ ἄνωθεν) which are known (only) to God and, among humans, to the one who is a friend of God, and for that reason are not given depiction (53d6–7).

This statement follows upon the *Timaeus*'s introduction of elementary triangles as elements or 'principles' of perceptible bodies (52c–d). What principles can be communicated 'to everyone', i.e. through writing, and who are the people for whom that is inappropriate cannot be specified for us as readers of the dialogues according to any general rule. The example just given provides us with a small insight into the way Plato leads the world of the senses back to intelligible principles; here he sets the limit to what can be communicated after the first step of the reduction which led to the field of geometry (that the 'even higher principles' denote, beyond elementary triangles, numbers is something which we can state with certainty thanks to Aristotle).[66] We cannot say whether Plato set down this limit once and for all; it is more probable that it was a question of discretion how much of his 'seed' he wanted to sow in an 'Adonis garden' and that he set the limit for each dialogue as he wrote it. Plutarch remarked that Plato was more inclined in his old age to state the principles he had in mind without concealment (*De*

Iside et Osiride 48, 370F), but we should add that the basic thought – that there are things which it is better not to reveal in writing, because if they are communicated prematurely they do not explain anything and are thus 'useless' – remains intact and unchanged from the metaphorical image of medical remedies in the *Charmides* through to the twelfth book of the *Laws*, where the significant concept of ἀπρόρρητα (*aprorrhêta*) is finally coined (968e).

17

SOME 'GAPS'

Another thing which remains unchanged is that one can never learn from the allusions to missing material with sufficient clarity what the content of the missing material consists of. We would never be able to discover what the 'even higher principles' beyond the elementary triangles are supposed to be if we were limited to this allusion alone in *Timaeus* 53d. In this case, as has been remarked, it is only the Aristotelian evidence on Plato's unwritten teachings which sheds the necessary light.[67] The same is true of the famous 'gap' at *Republic* 506d–e, where Socrates makes it unmistakably clear to his discussion-partner, Glaucon, that the nature (the τί ἐστιν) of the Good is not to be discussed because it is a topic which goes beyond the framework of the present conversation. Indeed, no less a scholar than Hans-Georg Gadamer has argued that the information meant here about the nature of the Good, namely that the Good is the One, lies 'implicitly in the structure of the *Republic* as well';[68] but if anyone wished to conclude that it is sufficient to analyse the structure of the *Republic* in order to see what Plato meant by the undefined τί ἐστιν of the Good, he would be the victim of a circular argument: for actually the only reason why we can extrapolate the equation One = Good even from the structure of the *Republic* 'indirectly' is because we have the direct information in Aristotle that the Academy equated the One itself with the Good itself, but thought that its nature (οὐσία) lay mainly in its being one (*Metaphysics* N4, 1091b13–15).

In the case of the 'gaps' which refer to the theory of principles in Plato's oral philosophy we can thus understand the meaning of the cross-reference only if the tradition outside Plato provides us with a key to it.

Fortunately, there is another type of 'gap'. In common with the first, it does not present a puzzle which might be solved from the text itself by acute analysis and precise observation of the wording, but once again is a case where the content of the missing material cannot be reconstructed without additional information provided by an authority outside the work in question. But, unlike the first type, here the information necessary for supplementing the sense can be found in other works *by Plato himself*. The value of these passages consists of the fact that they give us an authentically Platonic confirmation of our interpretation of the 'gaps': by means of them, and from within the Platonic œuvre itself and without recourse to the 'unwritten teachings' (which are attested only indirectly), we can verify and establish that Plato's 'gaps' are not vague promises but refer in a concrete way to sharply defined theories and that they are not essentially puzzles to be solved from within the text, but refer directly to philosophical conclusions presented elsewhere.

Several of these 'gaps' relate to the doctrine of the soul. Again, that is no surprise when one considers how important the theory of the soul is for Plato's ontology, epistemology, cosmology and ethics. In the *Phaedrus* Plato even states literally that a knowledge of the nature of the soul is not possible without the knowledge of the nature of the universe (270c). Correspondingly, the figure in the dialogues who makes the clearest statements on the nature of the soul, Timaeus of Locri, is described as the most expert man in matters of the nature of the universe (*Timaeus* 27a), and in fact in the course of his lecture he brings cosmology and the doctrine of the soul into the closest contact. Because the rich philosophical background of the theory of the soul could not be developed each time and because the final arguments would in any case involve the *archai* (which cannot be communicated to everybody), the relatively high number of 'gaps' in this context can be explained easily.

In the great myth about Eros in the *Phaedrus*, after proving the immortality of the soul on the basis that it is self-moving Plato comes to speak about its form (*idea* 246a). He says that to show what kind of thing it is would properly entail an 'entirely divine' and long explanation, and thus it will only be stated here in a briefer and 'human' explanation whom it resembles (246a4–6).

Scholars have believed that they had to conclude from the opposition of 'divine' and 'human' explanations that the shorter human one is all that is actually attainable by humans. But Plato nowhere considers the knowledge which is typical of gods to be closed to humans on *a priori* grounds – on the contrary, if a human realises the highest of his capabilities he becomes *philosophos*, because through his knowledge of the Ideas he comes near to God, who is *sophos*.

Therefore it is also stated in the *Timaeus* that the knowledge of the *archai*, which is a distinctive feature of God, is accessible to those among mortals whom God loves (53d), and similarly in the *Phaedrus* that through anamnesis the soul of the philosopher is always as close as it can be to the world of the Ideas, 'his closeness to which gives a god his divinity' (249c, trans. Rowe), and that the philosopher thereby becomes 'perfect'.

In fact, we can discover from the *Phaedrus* itself what an analysis of the nature of the soul would have to achieve if it were to offer more than the vivid comparison with a winged chariot described as a 'human' explanation at 246aff. Such an analysis would have to ask whether the soul is composed of one or several parts, and, if it consists of more than one part, what its capability (its *dynamis*) consists of in terms of action and passive suffering (270d1–7). It is clear that the myth did not confront these questions critically but answered them without formal argumentation but with the inspired verve of the poetic comparison. But it is equally clear that these questions can be tackled in a critical and reasoned way within the framework of the Platonic dialogues and that they were indeed so tackled, namely in the fourth book of the *Republic*. At 435eff. we find a carefully argued explanation why the soul is not to be considered as consisting of one part, why a distinction has to be made between precisely three 'parts' of the soul and where each of their capabilities lies.

Do we therefore have before us, in writing, the 'divine' explanation of the nature of the soul in the fourth book of the *Republic*? That would be too great a claim, since the theory of the soul offered there is itself heavily qualified (in a way that we shall consider in greater detail directly); but no judicious reader will be able to deny that the arguments of the fourth book of the *Republic* comply far better with the agenda of a philosophical psychology drawn from *Phaedrus* 270d (see also 271d), and in any case come closer to the 'divine' explanation than the beautiful image of the chariot of the soul.

Apart from possessing a deep knowledge of the nature of the soul, the dialectician, as the advocate of a rhetoric which is based on philosophical principles, particularly needs to know the nature of the things about which he wishes to impart the truth (*Phaedrus* 273d–274a; see also 277b–c). Here again there is a reference to a 'long detour' which has 'much effort' in store, but which in the end leads to our being able to speak and act in a way which is 'gratifying to the gods' (*Phaedrus* 273e4–5, e7–8, 274a2; trans. Rowe). The 'path' which Plato means here is the path or 'journey' (πορεία, *Republic* 532e3) of dialectic; as always, Plato represents it as a path which we can really tread, i.e. he presents a real possibility for mankind, and which leads to a strictly circumscribed goal which humans must reach in order to attain to their happiness. There is no room for doubt that this is the path of oral dialectic to which the dialogue makes reference, but it cannot be trodden in the medium of writing.

In the *Gorgias* Plato refers to his theory of the soul in a form which reveals far less of the 'form' (ἰδέα, *idea*) of the soul than the image of the tripartite chariot of the soul. Socrates' discussion-partner Callicles is, as we have already seen (p. 6f.), hindered by his blind egocentricity and compulsiveness from understanding the core principles of Socratic ethics: his biggest handicap is his primitive self-identification with his desires (491e–492c). Socrates confronts it with a totally different picture of mankind which he represents as the view of other anonymous 'wise men' (σοφοί), in order to underline its distance from Callicles' intellectual world. According to this view, the irrational people are those who are uninitiated (493a7): they do not know that life in the body (σῶμα) is like life in a grave (σῆμα) and that the continual satisfaction of the instincts and desires is nothing other than what the myth of the Danaids vividly expresses, namely an attempt to fill a leaky barrel with a sieve (492e8–493c3). In Socrates' understanding of the image the 'barrel' corresponds with a part of the soul: it is 'the part of the soul in which desires are located' (493a3, b1). The soul is thus a structured whole in which the 'sieve' serves the needs of the 'barrel'; but obviously this is true only of the way of life of irrational people and those who are controlled by their instincts, just as Callicles thinks that the only function of insight (φρόνησις, 492a2) is to serve the instincts. Taken together with Socrates' suggestion that Callicles choose the life of self-control instead of the life of the unbridled and basically unfulfillable satisfaction of the instincts (493c–d), Socrates' recourse to the myth of the Danaids means that the passions and instincts are not the entire soul but only one part, to which only irrational people subordinate insight, for they do not know that the soul knows of yet another life – the life of the rational soul in a state which is free of the body. Furthermore, since Callicles' ideal of excellence is measured against the system of the Platonic cardinal virtues (489e, 491c–e), which is, for its part, connected to the theory of the tripartite soul in the *Republic*, it is obvious that Callicles would above all else need enlightenment concerning the structure of the soul in order for him to be totally freed from his errors about himself and consequently about the type of life most worth striving for. Only in this way could he understand the meaning of 'having control over oneself' (αὐτὸν ἑαυτοῦ ἄρχειν, 491d8). But Callicles does not receive this enlightenment, obviously because his moral state precludes any cognitive progress. That essential things are intentionally kept out of the discussion here even though they are in fact essential for a valid analysis of the problems is indicated to Callicles (and the reader of the dialogue) by means of the image of the Mysteries: Socrates says scornfully that Callicles should be delighted to be initiated into the 'Greater Mysteries' before he has become acquainted with the 'Lesser Mysteries' (497c) – every reader of the time knew that that was inadmissible in the Eleusinian Mysteries, and yet Plato makes Socrates express the fact himself. Readers are meant to understand that they are not to expect an initiation into Plato's 'Greater Mysteries' here in the *Gorgias*.[69]

For Callicles, an introduction into the Platonic doctrine of the parts of the soul in the form it takes in *Republic* Book Four would itself have entailed a decisive step forwards. But for the character who represents the 'dialectician', Socrates, even this version is not at all the same as revealing the 'Greater Mysteries'. Abandoning the image of the Mysteries and reverting instead to prosaic clarity, he states, before he develops his theory with arguments, that the procedure that he has been following in his conversation with Glaucon and Adeimantus is insufficient for a 'precise' answer to the question of the parts of the soul: 'Be assured, Glaucon; in my opinion we shall never understand this precisely with the methods which we are now using in our discussions – for there is another path, one which is longer and more extensive, that leads to it.' (*Republic* 4, 435c9–d3).

In this way Plato limits the philosophical range of the reasoning behind the theory which is the basis of the doctrine of virtue and the design of the State.

But Plato does not leave things at this one reference. He refers back emphatically to the passage in Book Four when he prepares to introduce another basic theory. In the sixth book, when Socrates begins to explain why the philosophical rulers in the ideal State of the future will have to have a sound knowledge of the Good, he straight away recalls the decision, made in the fourth book, to treat the theory of the soul on a deliberately reduced level of argumentation (504a). Characteristically, the conversation-partner at first has no memory of it – one almost gets the impression here that Plato, on the basis of a superior psychological knowledge, wanted to caricature the inability to realise his dialogues' obvious self-limitations.

But Socrates remains insistent, and finally the same limitation is approved for the new theme of the Idea of the Good as well. The 'longer' way cannot be entered on at this precise point. Considered within the dramatic setting, this is because of the lack of training on the part of the conversation-partners (see 533a); seen from the perspective of the *Republic* as a book, it is because of the limits which writing imposes on philosophical communication. It is notable that, at the point where Socrates approaches the discussion of the 'highest object of learning' (the μέγιστον μάθημα, 503e, 504d–e, 505a), he stresses (504b–d) how inadequate it is to avoid the 'longer way' far more emphatically than in the fourth book. In the end he explains that he does not want to deal with the question of the nature of the Idea of the Good (506d–e), that even the image of the sun, given as a substitute, is incomplete in many ways and that in what follows he only wants to explain what is 'possible at the present moment' (ὅσα γ᾽ ἐν τῷ παρόντι δυνατόν, 509c9–10); both passages make it perfectly clear that explanations are not limited because the subject is incapable of being expressed, as has occasionally been maintained, but that Socrates does possess a 'view' on the Good, which, however, he will deliberately not disclose:

> But, my dear friends, let us leave aside for now the topic of what the Good in fact is; for I think that even my view on it is beyond our reach in our present attempt. (506d8–e3)
> . . . – Don't stop at all, he said, but once again explain the image of the sun, if you have (up till now) been leaving anything out.
> – Well, I said, I have been leaving out a great deal.
> – You shouldn't pass over even the least detail, he said.
> – I think [sc. that I'll pass over] a lot, I said; all the same, I shall not wilfully leave out whatever is feasible at this point. (509c5–10)

The meaning of Socrates' intention to explain only what is 'feasible at this point' is made clear from his refusal in the seventh book to explain the content and methods of dialectic in a brief sketch: 'You won't be able to follow me any further, my dear Glaucon – for my part, there won't be any lack of willingness' (533a1–2).

In Plato's major work, therefore, abandoning the 'longer way', which the *Phaedrus* knows of also (274a; see above, p. 68f.), has a bearing on the doctrine of the soul on the one hand and, on the other, on the philosophy of the Good and consequently the whole field of Platonic dialectic, which leads to the recognition of the final *archê*. As mentioned above (p. 66), supplementing the contents of this field can only be achieved in part from the indirect tradition. As far as the theme of the 'longer way', the doctrine of the soul, is concerned, however, Plato begins, in the *Republic* itself, to describe what is missing at least in outline, and thanks to a couple of statements in the *Timaeus* we can reach a clear and certain opinion on at least one central matter.

In the tenth book of the *Republic* Plato introduces in two steps a vitally important supplement to the psychological theory of his major work: first he proves the immortality of the soul, which has played no part up to this point (608c–611a); then he continues (I paraphrase 611a–612a): We must not think that the soul is constituted 'by its truest nature' (Bloom) as it has appeared to us up till now, as full of variety, irregularity and strife. Whatever is composed of many things and does not possess the best means of combining them can hardly be everlasting. One has to view the soul in its pure form, i.e. free of all the secondary accretion which it has gained from association with the body. One can recognise its 'old nature' (ἀρχαίαν φύσιν, 611d2) by looking at its love of wisdom, its *philosophia*: one can then see what it is in contact with and what it longs to associate with in view of its relationship to the divine and ever-existent. Observing it in such a way would reveal its 'true nature', whether it is multiform or uniform: as it is, however, we have observed the things which it experiences (πάθη) and the forms (εἴδη) it takes in human life.

Here, then, Plato places a future investigation of the soul in sharp contrast with the investigation which has so far been carried out in the dialogue. Both types of investigation are directed to the same question, namely whether the soul has parts and if so which: for the question of the soul's being multiform or uniform (612a4) means the same as the question in the fourth book, whether or not the soul exhibits the 'parts' which could be observed in the State as an enlarged model (435c4–6). But only the future examination will reveal the 'old' or 'true' nature of the soul and be able to say of *that* whether it has more parts or only one.

The psychology of the *Republic* is thus emphatically one which is of the here and now and, so to speak, 'empirical'. Its results are thoroughly valid for the realm in which they were achieved, as is specifically emphasised (611c6, 612a5–6). But it has no access to the most important thing: to the 'true nature' of its object.

If we look at the wording alone, we must say that the question of the multiformity or uniformity of the true soul is left open (612a4); only the complete and final examination of the soul, which is missing in the dialogue, will give a decisive answer. This apparent openness has led scholars either to attribute the wrong answer to Plato or even to explain that he himself still did not know what the solution would look like.

In reality, Plato's view of the true nature of the soul can be learnt not only from this passage but also from others in the *Republic*, but unfortunately not with the explicitness needed to command general assent. That the 'true nature of the soul' could be multiform in the same sense as the soul in this corporeal life is something which is already excluded by the sharp contrast between the two ways of describing the soul. In particular, the statement that the true soul is related to the divine and the eternally existent shows clearly that only the λογιστικόν (*logistikon*), or the highest part of the tripartite soul, can be meant by it. The notion that it could 'entirely follow' the eternally existent, i.e. the world of Ideas (611e4), points in the same direction – especially if one includes what is said about the 'relationship' and the inclinations of the three parts of the soul in the ninth book (see 585bff.): since the *logistikon* alone is directed towards 'what is eternally the same, the immortal and the truth' and consequently it alone assimilates itself to this realm (see 500c), only it is called 'the divine' in the human make-up (589d1, e4, 590d1). It is thereby actually implied that only the *logistikon* can be immortal, since the other two parts of the soul are directed towards mortal things and 'follow' them. A passage in the seventh book is even clearer; there it is said that the virtue of 'being rational' (of φρονῆσαι) is – in contrast with the other virtues which are almost like bodily virtues – the function 'of something more divine', 'which never loses its strength' (518d–e).

The modification of the doctrine of the soul which is the outcome of these passages is therefore as follows: the only immortal part of the tripartite soul is the rational soul, the *logistikon*; thus it alone reveals the indestructible 'old' or 'true' nature of the soul, while the two other parts of the soul in the fourth book were indeed correctly separated from one another and from the *logistikon*, but by their very nature are nothing other than a transitory accretion which is caused by the 'true' soul's association with the body.

But precisely this picture of the human soul can be formed from the dialogue the *Timaeus*. Only the rational soul is created by the Demiurge, or 'mixed together', as Plato puts it (35a, 41d): it alone is therefore indestructible. The two other parts of the soul are 'built on' by subordinate deities as mortal additions (69c–d); in accordance with their nature they are directed at mortal things, namely passions and ambition (90b), while the *logistikon* has the task of becoming like the order and harmony of the heavens by a rational comprehension of the revolutions of the universe, 'in accord with its old nature' (90c–d, κατὰ τὴν ἀρχαίαν φύσιν, d5; cf. *Republic* 611d2).

This dichotomous structure of the soul, with its ontological division between the immortal and the two mortal parts, is also clearly mentioned by Plato in the *Politicus* (309c) and in the *Laws* (713c), and is obviously assumed in the *Phaedo*. But here, at the conclusion of the *Republic*, we discover no explicit description of this structure, and still less any explanation of the nature of the soul from its connection with the intelligible – presumably because such an explanation would not have been possible without further statements on the world of the Ideas, while the discussion-partners would not have been able to cope with the 'longer way'. Even the clearer passages which I have cited do not let us understand with complete clarity what the result of such a revelation of the 'true nature' of the soul might consist of. (To be sure, the remaining uncertainty relates only to the nature and constitution of the rational soul; there is no further room for doubt that the 'true nature' denotes the *logistikon* and that only this can be immortal.) When Plato talks of 'becoming like' and 'relationship', he presumably does not simply mean identity; perhaps he was thinking of a definition by means of which the rational soul would be assigned to the middle ontological realm, mentioned by Aristotle, between the Ideas and the world of the senses to which mathematical objects belong as well.[70] The famous 'mixture' of the world soul (which is pure rational soul) according to mathematical ratios in the *Timaeus* (35a–36d) in any case suggests this possibility.[71]

The *Timaeus* perhaps also clarifies the formulation, which might momentarily seem disconcerting, that future examination would show the true nature of the soul, 'whether it is multiform or uniform, or whatever its composition might be' (εἴτε πολυειδὴς εἴτε μονοειδής, εἴτε ὅπῃ ἔχει καὶ ὅπως, 612a4). It is unlikely that Plato was uncertain of what the result would be. If one proceeds on the basis of the doctrine of the partition of the soul in the fourth book of the *Republic* it is unambiguous that the answer will be that the true old nature of the soul is uniform, μονοειδής, because the two other 'parts' (εἴδη) are oriented towards mortal things and as a consequence are themselves mortal. The fact that Plato leaves it at an 'open' formulation could be precisely because he is no longer thinking of

74

the partition of the soul in the sense of the fourth book, but already of the 'mixture' of the rational soul out of different 'parts' – even if these 'parts' finally prove themselves in the *Timaeus* to be something quite different from the 'parts' of the tripartite soul.

We should not doubt the importance of the qualification to which Plato subjects his theory of the soul in *Republic* 611a–612a. Inasmuch as the content of future, more precise examination can, at least in its central point, be supplemented with total certainty from other dialogues, we have a guarantee that by the 'longer way' Plato is referring to concrete results of his philosophical activity, as well as in those passages where he has not made such a means of checking possible for us.

Republic 611a–612a is remarkable in yet another respect: we have established that this text, by referring to a more precise psychology which is not yet available, anticipates the contents of that examination by allusions. This brings us back to the question which is so important for the interpretation of Plato, the question of the role of the allusions and the hints for which the reader must supply a content. Must we value the importance of the allusions more highly than we have done so far? Before we attempt an answer to this question (see below, Chapter 19), let us turn to a further text of Plato's which by means of allusions refers to different results which are of more basic importance than those present in the text itself.

18

THE DOCTRINE OF
ANAMNESIS AND DIALECTIC
IN THE *EUTHYDEMUS*

In the *Euthydemus* the reader is confronted again and again with apparently pointless, deceptive conclusions with which Dionysodorus and Euthydemus would like to confuse their partners. Several of these deceptive conclusions make good sense, however, if they are interpreted against the background of Plato's view of learning and the doctrine of anamnesis.[72]

First of all, the question is put to the young Clinias: who learns, the wise or the ignorant (οἱ σοφοὶ ἢ οἱ ἀμαθεῖς, 275d4)? The answer 'the wise' is refuted, whereupon Clinias opts for the ignorant, which is however likewise refuted (275d3–276c7). So far, all this feels like a sophistic game, and for the characters in the drama, Euthydemus and Dionysodorus, this is precisely the purpose. But one realises immediately that more is involved for the author Plato as soon as one brings *Symposium* 203eff. and *Lysis* 218a to bear: according to these passages the learner is neither someone who has knowledge nor someone who does not. But this neither–nor position, the only way the two refutations would make sense, does not appear in the *Euthydemus*, as little as the related concepts of Eros and philosophy.

In the case of the second question, too – does one learn what one knows or what one does not know? – both possible answers are refuted (276d7–277c7). In the *Meno* precisely this conclusion – that one can learn neither what one knows nor what one does not know – occurs as an 'eristic argument', which Socrates destroys there by expounding the theory of anamnesis (80df.). But this solution does not occur in the *Euthydemus*.

None the less, it shines through clearly in a later passage: the eristicians prove that whoever knows something knows everything (293b–e), that everyone knows everything (294a–e) and that everyone always knew everything (294e–296d). What might sound here like arrant nonsense is transparent and meaningful against the background of the *Meno*: from one 'recollection' the person with understanding can seek after everything, since all things are bound together by one relationship: further, since every soul has seen the Ideas before entering the body, every human being potentially knows everything; and in view of the knowledge of geometry which Socrates elicits from the uneducated slave of Meno one can see that indeed everyone has potentially known everything (*Meno* 81c–d, 85d–86b; see *Phaedrus* 249b on the viewing of the Ideas before birth).

The two eristicians prove, further, that their own father is at the same time the father of their discussion-partner, but beyond that the father of all human beings, indeed of all living creatures, including all sea-urchins, pigs and dogs (298b–e). This strange 'relationship' between humans and animals of all kinds is however presumably meant as a caricaturing variation on the tenet which contains the ontological basis of the doctrine of anamnesis: 'since the whole of nature is related' (ἅτε γὰρ τῆς φύσεως ἁπάσης συγγενοῦς οὔσης, *Meno* 81c9).

It is therefore plain that several of the deceptive conclusions in the *Euthydemus* are conceived with the theory of anamnesis in mind. But this theory is not discussed there, or even mentioned. The word 'soul' (295b4) might perhaps remind us that the Platonic doctrine of the soul is the background which could give sense and meaning to the silly games of the eristicians. But this allusion – if it is one – can only be understood by people who already know something about the Platonic doctrine of anamnesis and the soul.

There is even an allusion to the doctrine of the Ideas (which was almost to be expected in view of the fundamental connectedness of the theory of anamnesis and the Ideas). The problem of the relationship between particular and Idea is obviously one with which Socrates is familiar (301a2–4); for him, 'the Beautiful itself' is separate from the beautiful particular instance, but the latter is beautiful because of the 'presence' of the Beautiful (note πάρεστιν, 301a4). On the level represented by the eristician Dionysodorus, the conclusion reached from all this is that Socrates would become an ox through the presence of an ox (301a5).

Since the theory of the Ideas in the *Republic* is connected with a detailed conception of the relationship of the branches of knowledge to one another, it is no surprise that this theme also is mentioned. Mathematics, as we are told at 290c–d, cannot be the sought-after highest branch, since production (or acquisition) and use must coincide in the latter, while mathematics leaves what it achieves to dialectic just as a general hands over a conquered city to politics. This view of the relationship of mathematics and philosophy is not prepared for by anything in the *Euthydemus* and remains incomprehensible even in the framework of the dialogue; it is only when one ventures beyond the dialogue and includes *Republic* 510cff., 531cff. that the meaning is made clear. Thus Plato presupposes more than he expresses.

In the search for the decisive highest 'branch of knowledge' or 'art', the art of speech-writing (ἡ λογοποιικὴ τέχνη, 289c7) is also considered and rejected. The reason for its rejection is the reference to 'certain speech-writers' (289d2), in whose case the production and use of their products is separated; they write speeches but do not deliver them, while their clients indeed use these speeches but could not compose them themselves. It is accepted that it is not this art of rhetoric which can be the highest art for bestowing happiness – and yet *Socrates* had thought that he would find it 'somewhere' in this area (289d8–e1). One can, however, take it from these striking formulations that there might be *another* 'art of rhetoric' which would fulfil the criteria for the 'branch of knowledge sought after' (e1). What is meant is obviously the aspect of dialectic which is developed in the *Phaedrus*, namely dialectic as an ideal art of rhetoric. Dialectic is there understood as oral philosophical inquiry, in the case of which the dialectician indeed first produces the 'speeches' in conversation with the appropriate addressee but simultaneously uses them in accordance with his knowledge of the soul and of the subject.[73] In the *Phaedrus* we also read that the logoi of dialectic engender the happiness, *eudaimonia*, which humans are capable of (277a3).

In general, one gets the impression that in the *Euthydemus* a rich philosophical background is present, which however shapes the train of thought only in a covert way, without dominating it. Such important components of Plato's philosophy as the doctrine of anamnesis and the Ideas and the theory of dialectic are present in substance, but they are nowhere named clearly, let alone reviewed in a coherent manner or even argued for. They are thus not noticed by the dialogue's discussion-partners, and might never have been noticed by us as readers either if we were not explicitly instructed by other dialogues about the theories concerned.

19

THE IMPORTANCE OF THE
ALLUSIONS FOR READING
PLATO

We now have sufficient examples at hand to enable us to treat the question of the allusions in Plato afresh.[74] The question is of course not whether there are allusions and references which are left to the actively engaged reader to express – it is obvious that there are such things in Plato; but, since there are such things in other authors too, as we shall see, we must, in order to find what is specifically Platonic about Plato's philosophical writing, inquire more closely what status he assigned to writing allusively.

Up till now we have found no evidence that Plato believed that he might come close to oral philosophical inquiry in writing by a sophisticated use of subtle allusions, indirect references and coded clues. That was the naive belief of Friedrich Schleiermacher, who combined it with the antiesoteric conviction that, through the art of 'indirect' communication, reserving essential parts of his philosophy for the realm of orality was unnecessary for Plato. Yet writing remains basically reliant on oral supplementation by 'things of greater value' (*timiôtera*). It is a modern misapprehension that written allusions can fulfil the function of this oral supplementation; we shall have more to say about it later. But first let me demonstrate by means of different types of allusions and references that they do not at all function in Plato as rivals of direct communication, whether it be written or spoken.

(a) The most simple form of allusion is pointing out what is meant by means of a reference in the form of a quotation. We find this type at *Phaedrus* 276e2–3, where Plato names 'story-telling' (μυθολογεῖν) about justice and related themes as an example of the philosopher's 'play' in writing. Since the *Republic* deals with justice and the other virtues and since it describes itself as a μυθολογεῖν in two places (376d, 501e), there can be no doubt that Plato here refers

79

to his own major work as a case of written philosophical 'play'. But it is left to the reader's resources to recognise the allusion for what it is and to draw the correct conclusion from it, namely that Plato's own works are included in the critique of everything that is written.

So isn't the most important question of the critique of writing answered by a mere allusion? Not at all. For the question whether or not Plato's dialogues are subject to the critique of writing is one which is relevant only to the modern theory of the dialogues which is vitally interested in exempting the dialogues from the critique on the grounds of its antiesoteric presuppositions. For Plato, that was not a question: he directed his critique against writing (γραφή) in general. And for the reader who is not inclined to twist the clear implication of the text because of modern prejudices, it is stated directly, not only in allusive terms, that the critique refers to the dialogues as well, when it refers to *everything* that has been written down. A reader who has grasped this has grasped the essential point – whether or not he recognises the unobtrusive reference to the *Republic* is pretty immaterial in comparison.

It is entirely understandable that the unobtrusive reference should have been discovered quite late – in fact only in 1961, by W. Luther.[75] What is really amazing is the fact that the completely unambiguous reference continues to be neglected or treated as uncertain by most commentators even after it has been discovered. It only goes to show how right Plato was: nothing 'clear and permanent' can be expressed by means of writing; even in the case of evaluating such a simple and 'certain' allusion considerable room remains for subjective judgment. Why should we accept that Plato of all people staked so much on the unambiguity of allusions? The critique of writing shows clearly enough that he had long since shed the naivety necessary for that.

(b) In connection with the 'even higher *archai*' which are referred to at *Timaeus* 53d but are not explained there, we had the opportunity to recall a passage in the *Laws* in which the origin (γένεσις, *genesis*) of all things is mentioned (above, n. 67). The text reads as follows:

> What process must occur for things to come into being in each case? It is clearly possible only when a beginning (*archê*) is present and takes on an accretion and so reaches a second stage of development (μετάβασιν), and from this reaches the next until it arrives at the third, when it can provide some perception of itself for creatures capable of perception.

> Everything originates by means of such change and transfer-
> ence; everything has true existence as long as it endures in
> this way, but as soon as it changes into another state it is
> entirely destroyed.
>
> (*Laws* 10, 894a1–8)

No one will be able to deny that the passage 'must at first be regarded as puzzling', as Konrad Gaiser put it.[76] That is also the case when the context of the passage in the tenth book of the *Laws* is examined carefully. As Konrad Gaiser has shown, true clarity is only achieved when the evidence for the unwritten theory of principles is taken into consideration; the passage then proves itself as an inten-tionally cryptic representation of a mathematical theory concerning the transition from the first to the second to the third dimension which Plato used as a model for explaining ontological facts.[77]

Can one say here that the essential points are conveyed allusively? No, because basically nothing is 'conveyed' here, at least not to the reader who has not been given prior information *from another source*; without the sources which Gaiser brings into discussion our passage would remain indefinite to the point of obscurity and would be at the mercy of subjective interpretations. And the explanation of *gen-esis* by means of the three dimensions is not 'the essential point' for what the tenth book of the *Laws* is actually intended to show, namely that a reasoning world-soul reigns in the universe. However, the fact that the contents of the philosophical education of the State's directors belongs to the *aprorrhêta* which it would be point-less to convey prematurely is something which the reader learns not through cryptic allusion but through direct statement at the end of the work (968e; see above, p. 62).

(c) When we explained the philosophical insights which appear from 'behind' the confusing and apparently absurd trains of thought in the *Euthydemus* (Chapter 18 above), it was necessary to emphasise that none of this dialogue's 'riddles' would be solvable without our knowing the uncoded exposition of the doctrine of anamnesis and of the concept of dialectic in the *Meno*, the *Phaedo* and the *Republic*. The 'riddles' of the *Euthydemus* are thus not at all puzzles in the sense of the archaic literary genre of the *ainos*, the chief charm of which resides in the fact that the audience deduces the meaning from the text itself without external help. For Oedipus, the puzzle of the sphinx had to be solvable without specific information which only he had at his disposal: his entire fame as a puzzle-solver would have been forfeited if he had approached the task under special conditions. On the other hand, the 'puzzle' that everybody knows everything and has already always known everything (*Euthydemus* 294a–e, 294e–296d) is solvable only if we possess prior information which is specifically Platonic; but without this it would be what the unprimed reader takes it to be, namely arrant nonsense.

It is not by means of indefinite allusions that Plato signals here that particular and important material lies in the background, but by means of the dramaturgical device of interrupting the narration of the dialogue; we shall deal with this subject in Chapter 20.

(d) When we discussed the 'gap' at *Republic* 611/12, we inclined to the view that the result of the more precise analysis of the soul which is not conducted in the dialogue can nonetheless be gleaned from a few hints in the text (above, pp. 72–75). Does the allusion here accordingly have the function of communicating the essential point in a veiled way?

Indeed, Plato does not say 'The "true nature" of the soul is uniform, for in its "purified" form the soul is identical with the highest of its three "parts", the *logistikon*.' However, if one considers that this conclusion results very simply from the statement that the true nature of the soul can be discovered from its *philosophia*, its association and relationship with the divine and eternally existent (611e), one asks oneself in what sense we can talk about a 'coded' communication. It is, rather, a matter of simply remembering earlier conclusions in the dialogue (see above, p. 72f.). Significantly, the reader's simple 'task' of combining earlier material with the present topic has not led to the necessary 'clarity and certainty' of knowledge; instead, it has been disputed that Plato here wishes to limit immortality to the *logistikon*.[78]

It is decisive for the evaluation of the passage that the question left open at 611/12 can only be answered from the *Republic* itself in so far as the 'true nature' of the soul is to be equated with one of the three parts of the soul. On the other hand, what might be meant by the multiformity of the true soul itself cannot even be guessed from the *Republic*; it is only the direct information about the ingredients of the 'mixture of the soul' (*Timaeus* 35a–36d) which can give us an idea of the more advanced ontological analysis of the soul.

In summary, we can state that Plato makes use of the most divergent types of allusions, suggestions and references, but that he nowhere reveals any intention to assign a central role to the literary device of allusion in philosophical communication.[79]

Heraclitus' famous comment that the god of the Delphic oracle 'neither states nor conceals but gives signs'[80] is an outstanding description of the way that oracles and enigmatic speech (αἶνος, αἴνιγμα) communicated. But Plato had far outgrown the archaic literary minor forms of oracle and αἶνος; he can use them on occasion, and he uses them in a masterly way, but always to subservient and supplementary purposes. If one wants to understand his actual intention as a philosophical writer, one must first and foremost consider why he adopted the new major literary form of prose-drama, and ask with what dramaturgical means he makes it clear what matters to him. But the criterion for judging all interpretations is and remains the critique of writing.

But the spirit of the critique of writing is contravened in two ways by the modern theory of the dialogues, which ascribes the decisive function of philosophical education to the written allusions – in such a way as to make any esoteric oral philosophy of principles unnecessary through them. First, the modern theory forgets that according to Plato 'clarity and certainty (permanence)' of knowledge cannot be ensured by writing (*Phaedrus* 275c6–7, 277d7–8); its view that necessarily indefinite allusions can surmount this obstacle, which is inherent in the nature of writing, is based on a naive optimism which Plato never shared and which has been completely refuted by the history of the reception of Plato's works. Second, it overlooks the fact that selecting the 'appropriate soul', which for Plato is the prerequisite of significant philosophical instruction – in any other circumstance the philosopher will remain silent – is fundamentally impossible when writing is used. The coded allusion can be decoded by any reader who has the necessary intelligence. An example of this is Alcibiades, who has long been lost to the cause of philosophy, and who announces in the *Symposium* that one only has to 'open' the Socratic logoi to have everything one needs to become good and virtuous (*Symposium* 221d–222a).[81] But Plato does not just demand intellectual capability from the 'appropriate soul'; he also demands an inner affinity to the cause of philosophy, an affinity which also includes the presence in the soul of the cardinal virtues in the full philosophical sense (*Republic* 487a; see also the *Seventh Letter* 344a). One must ask oneself in amazement how this enormous gap, which separates modern confidence in the educational function of the allusions and the 'indirect mode of communication' from Plato's view of a philosophical use of writing, could have been overlooked for so long. It was perhaps only possible because from the very beginning, that is, since Friedrich Schleiermacher, consideration of the Platonic dialogues has been guided by antiesoteric wishful thinking. Schleiermacher, in fact, believed that it was Plato's aim to organise the use of writing in such a way that it might achieve almost the same as oral communication for imparting knowledge. In the *Phaedrus*, which Schleiermacher considered an early work, Plato is not yet supposed to have had any hope of achieving that, but later succeeded in doing so,[82] so that he 'did not end up believing that philosophy was so comprehensively incapable of being imparted'.[83] For Schleiermacher, then, Plato adopted a point of view in the critique of writing which he later overcame. This was the belief on which Schleiermacher based his theory of the dialogues, which still is credited today by many people. In the meantime, it is now known that the *Phaedrus* is a relatively late work, not written before 370 BC, and that it contains Plato's well-considered, final view of the proper use of writing for philosophy. Thus we can also dismiss as un-Platonic the modern theory of the Platonic dialogues, which is based on false presuppositions and which wishes to load on to the allusions and references in the text the task which only oral philosophical inquiry can fulfil.[84]

20

PLATO'S DRAMATIC TECHNIQUE

Some examples

As mentioned above, understanding the dialogues does not have to be directed by the hermeneutics of the archaic literary miniature forms of the oracle (χρησμός) and riddle (αἶνος, αἴνιγμα), but must start from the more developed large-scale form of drama. In fact, Plato has all the techniques of developed dramaturgy at his disposal, and he knows how to deploy them judiciously in order to present his concept of philosophy. A complete description of Plato's dramatic techniques is not my intention here: any such attempt would require a second book of at least the length of this one. All that can be offered here are a few examples which can demonstrate the old insight that the form of the Platonic dialogues is not a superficial thing, but is essential to their content. Indeed, many interpreters of recent generations have declared their support for this insight, but that has remained mainly lip-service; the unity of content and form, announced so programmatically, has rarely had any concrete consequences for interpreting Plato. Many an astonishing insight can be won here by an accurate observation of Plato's literary methods and an examination of them in the light of the critique of writing.[85]

(a) The continuous 'plot'

In general, the fact that the Platonic dialogues as a rule have a continuous 'plot' is seldom recognised. One method by which Plato keeps this plot in the reader's mind is the repetition of motifs.

In the *Euthydemus*, as has already been mentioned (p. 13f.), the continuous plot consists of the exposure of the eristicians Euthydemus and Dionysodorus as non-esotericists, and for Plato that means as non-philosophers. Step by step it is shown that they are not storing up any 'things of greater value' with which they might be able to support their logos when challenged. The motif by means of which this plot is furthered and divided into stages is that of 'concealment' on the one hand and the opposition of 'play' and 'seriousness' on the other. Socrates' tactic consists of viewing the eristic nonsense with which Euthydemus and Dionysodorus want to show off their brilliance as their 'play', and of challenging them again and again to come out with their 'seriousness', which they must still be keeping hidden. When it is established once and for all that they have nothing more valuable than their cheap fallacies, Socrates sarcastically advises them to keep on withholding their knowledge in such a fine esoteric manner.

Interpreters have not failed to notice that in this dialogue 'Socrates' has at his disposal the doctrines of the Ideas and anamnesis as well as the Platonic concept of dialectic.[86] Yet it has not been understood what this fact means in the context of the dialogue, because critics have not thought to bring Socrates' perceptible background knowledge into relation with the continuous plot. But if one assesses Socrates' head-start from the perspective of the plot, and he does indeed ironically conceal it in the dialogue, it all at once becomes clear that he is himself precisely what he categorises the eristicians as being: a person with knowledge who consciously withholds his 'seriousness'. The plot of the dialogue can now be formulated as follows: the true esotericist, Socrates, exposes two charlatans by proving that they do not have any withheld 'seriousness' at their command at all; in an ironical reversal of reality he depicts them as esotericists. What is scorned is thus not the esoteric withholding of knowledge, but precisely the inability to exercise it. In positive terms, that means that the message of the *Euthydemus*, which is discernible only if one takes the leitmotif and the continuous plot into consideration, is that the true philosopher must be an esotericist.

In the *Charmides* the continuous plot consists of a kind of 'conversion' of the young Charmides, or of his sudden and unconditional devotion to Socrates, the ideal teacher. The motif that is combined with this plot is that of the 'medication' and the 'charm' which must be performed before the medication is applied.[87] The theme of the dialogue is the virtue of self-control.

The connection between plot, leitmotif and theme is, in brief, as follows. At the end of the dialogue Charmides decides in favour of Socrates as his teacher, which is doubtless a sign of the self-control which is already present in his soul as a natural tendency. But the actual decision rests with Socrates: he himself points out that it is up to him whether to release the 'incantation' or not (*Charmides* 156a). He could even apply the 'medication' directly, but the warning of his Thracian teacher discourages him from being seduced in any way into passing on the 'medication' without a prior 'incantation' (157b–c). As a teacher, then, Socrates needs the virtue of self-control on his own account, and he proves that he possesses it by withholding his deeper philosophical knowledge (his *pharmakon*) in the interests of proper instruction, for as long as it takes the preparatory conversations (the *epôdê*) to make the student ready for it. The weaving of leitmotif, plot and theme again shows that the true philosopher must be capable of esoteric reticence.

Third, we must analyse the continuous plot in the *Republic* more closely.[88] It consists of the attempt by a few friends to 'compel' Socrates to impart his views on justice, the best State, and finally on the Good and on dialectic as the way to the Idea of the Good. The motif which articulates the plot and which is varied again and again throughout the whole dialogue can be found on the first page of the work: the friends wish to 'keep hold of' Socrates and not to 'let him go' under any circumstances; he on the other hand thinks that he can quietly convince the friends to let him be (*Republic* 327a–c). Right at the beginning, therefore, the situation makes it clear that the others need the wisdom of Socrates, while he himself can even imagine withdrawing from the conversation. However, he gives in for the moment and the friends succeed in inducing him to expound on important matters: he is prepared, from Book Two onwards, 'to come to the aid' of justice (and thereby of his own logos in support of justice in Book One as well). He is not only prepared but also brilliantly competent; he introduces truly 'more valuable things' into the discussion, things which far transcend the intellectual framework of Book One and lead to more and more fundamental questions. But, as the discussion comes step by step closer to the principles (*archai*), there is a decrease in Socrates' inclination to open up to the others, until he can at last calmly convince them to 'let him go' in expounding his views on the Good and the methods and content of dialectic: his statement that Glaucon would not be able to follow him any more in that field (533a) is accepted by Glaucon without protest.

Thus the plot of the *Republic* began as a symbolic trial of strength: Socrates' friends threatened in jest to drag him into conversation even against his will (327c). But in the end the dialectician is revealed as the winner in the trial of strength. The others have to accept that it has to be left to Socrates to decide freely how much he imparts of his philosophical knowledge. Socrates makes it unmistakably clear that imparting his views is determined by whether or not the partner fulfils certain requirements, or, to put it another way, that his method is to proceed with philosophical knowledge on a basis which is strictly related to the addressee, or is 'esoteric'. Anyone who understands the plot of the *Republic* also understands that Plato had more to say about the Good as the highest principle than he wrote down in the book. Even without Aristotle's information we may know for certain, on the basis of Plato's major work alone, that there was an oral Platonic theory of principles.

(b) Interruptions in the narrative of the dialogues

Interrupting the narrative of the dialogue by means of the framing dialogue is a special dramaturgical device which Plato uses on occasion. Thus, in terms of form, the *Euthydemus* is a report by Socrates to Crito of a conversation which he had the day before with two eristicians in the Lyceum. In the course of the report we learn that the young Clinias had said of the art of dialectic that it was taking over the 'booty' of mathematics in the same way that politics takes over the booty of military strategy, for example a conquered city (290c–d).[89] In this assessment a certain relationship between mathematics and dialectic is implied which can only be understood in the light of the epistemology of the *Republic* (510cff., 531cff.), and seems like a foreign body within the *Euthydemus*, where the reader is not given any preparation for the conclusion.

In order to highlight the importance of recognising that mathematics is subordinate to dialectic, Plato interrupts the narrative of the dialogue and makes Crito ask whether the young Clinias said such a clever thing – if it was he, he needs no further human instruction (290e). To our amazement, Socrates is not willing to guarantee that it was Clinias; it might also have been Ctesippus. But when Crito is not prepared to accept that from him either, Socrates expresses the assumption that perhaps 'one of the higher beings' who happened to be present at just that moment had introduced the insight (291a4). We do not have to puzzle for long over whose voice the unrecognised god used. What is certain is that with dialectic the realm of what is 'higher', of the 'divine' philosophy, is reached. Thus Plato places no trust in the comprehensibility of his brief allusion to his epistemology, but deploys the much clearer dramatic device of interrupting the narrative of the dialogue in order to make it clear to the reader that behind the dialogue philosophical riches exist which are not made explicit but which are related to the matters discussed explicitly in such a way as the realm of the divine is related to that of the human.

The narration of the dialogue is interrupted in the *Phaedo* as well, twice in fact (as we saw above, p. 56f.). The reader's attention is thereby drawn to the importance of the 'support' which the philosopher must be capable of bringing to his own logos. The support that Socrates is in fact able to bring shows in an exemplary way that the philosopher *cannot*, as is often assumed, remain at the level of the logos which is to be defended. The two interruptions underline this state of affairs and thus, in combination with the theme of ascent from hypothesis to hypothesis, make it comprehensible why the support which transcends the case in point must be the central structural principle of the Platonic dialogues in general.

(c) Change of discussion-partner

In several dialogues Socrates' first discussion-partner is replaced in the course of the conversation, mostly, but not always, by a person of like mind. The change of persons often betokens a change in the level of argumentation and is standardly associated with a case of 'supporting the logos'.

In the *Gorgias*, the great sophist after whom the dialogue is named is questioned by Socrates in connection with the object and aims of his art (τέχνη). Socrates treats him politely; it is only his student Polus whom he presses with harder and more basic questions: when Polus shows that he is not up to the discussion, Callicles enters the conversation as a representative of political rhetoric.

The sequence of the discussion-partners can be explained in the light of the critique of writing. The dialectician can pass on to the appropriate student the capability to support the logos and thereby the originator of the logos (*Phaedrus* 276e–277a). If Gorgias and two of his followers are questioned, it means that Gorgias is being tested to see whether he is the true teacher of philosophy. It becomes evident that neither the teacher nor the students are capable of bringing philosophically well-founded support to their logos. The examination of Gorgias' position indeed reveals its deeper bases; it is just that these bases do not consist of 'things of greater value' (*timiôtera*). What becomes clear in the case of Callicles is the brutal negation of all ethics in the name of the so-called 'right of the stronger'. Thus the twofold change of persons in the *Gorgias* in one sense results in an ascending line, inasmuch as the discussion leads to more and more fundamental questions, and the dramatic tension of the argument continuously rises. In a charming way this ascending line intersects with a counter-movement in so far as the opposing position becomes less and less respectable in terms of its content, and sinks deeper and deeper.

Plato uses the same dramaturgical technique in the first book of the *Republic* with the sequence Cephalus, Polemarchus and Thrasymachus, just as the two figures Thrasymachus and Callicles appear to be two attempts at giving the same material dramatic shape. In the case of the *Republic* the discussion does not stop with the refutation of the negatively characterised opponent. After Thrasymachus' definition of justice as the 'advantage of the stronger' has been rejected without its real nature (its τί ἐστιν) having been discussed, the conversation could have come to its end; and in fact it is ended as far as the discussion-partner Thrasymachus is concerned.

But at the beginning of the second book the brothers Glaucon and Adeimantus make their appearance. In long speeches (358b–362c, 362e–367e) they renew Thrasymachus' attack on justice. Nevertheless, the discussion with them, which fills Books Two to Ten of the *Republic*, has no similarity to the discussion of Thrasymachus. The difference lies in the characters of the discussion-partners: while Thrasymachus attacks the traditional concept of justice out of inner conviction, Glaucon and Adeimantus want merely to provoke a thoroughgoing refutation by means of their arguments for injustice. They are personally convinced of the superiority of justice but do not possess the arguments necessary for defending it; this is something they would rather hear from Socrates.

Socrates, who had already thought that he had finished with the conversation (357a), now embarks on a discussion of quite another kind, for the sake of the brothers Glaucon and Adeimantus: in the place of the aporetic discussion, which consciously left open the τί ἐστιν of the matter discussed (347e, 354b) and was unambiguous only in refuting the incorrect view of justice, we now have the constructive conversation which sets forth an unexpected wealth of positive statements and arguments and finally, in the excursus on the doctrine of the soul, even reaches a definition of justice (443c–e). Yet both conversations – and this is of extreme importance – are held on the same day before the same circle of people, the one directly after the other. What is clearly expressed by this dramaturgical ordering is this: Plato gives us to understand that, in reality, behind the aporias of the dialogues on the virtues, which ostensibly cannot define the virtues of bravery, piety, self-control and justice, there stands the *Republic*'s system of the doctrine of the soul, the State and the virtues; and at the same time he shows that expounding such *timiôtera* can only succeed if it is desired by discussion-partners who bring with them the character-traits required for such instruction. Excluding inappropriate partners, however, has nothing to do with secrecy: Thrasymachus can attend the ensuing discussion, but is no longer the addressee. The discussion with him got stuck in the aporetic front courtyard of philosophy, whereas, for Glaucon and Adeimantus, Socrates is prepared to reveal the τί ἐστιν of justice. But the type of philosophical communication which is strictly addressee-related or esoteric is preserved even in their case, as we have already seen (see above, p. 87): they are not equipped for the τί ἐστιν of the Good and thus are not told Socrates' view of it (506e).

The use of the dramaturgical device of changing the discussion-partner in the *Symposium* is clearly different from these two cases. Whereas Polus and Callicles in the *Gorgias* and Glaucon and Adeimantus in the *Republic* are present from the beginning, Alcibiades breaks into the company of the symposiasts after the speeches on Eros have already reached their peak in Socrates' speech on Diotima (*Symposium* 212c). Indeed, the picture which the drunken Alcibiades draws of Socrates' character itself brings a second peak in the dialogue, but in the meantime the theme has shifted from the nature of Eros to the realisation of the philosophical Eros in the person of Socrates.

Alcibiades' report is totally shaped by personal experience. It becomes clear that Alcibiades was a person who had had the talent for philosophy and thus had been 'erotically' courted by Socrates for a while. But his unstable character made it impossible for him to hand himself over totally to Socrates' philosophical guidance; finally, he drifted away entirely from his influence. Thus Alcibiades gives fragments of a philosophical autobiography which show him as one called to philosophy but in the end not up to this calling. Alcibiades is the young philosopher who has not fulfilled the expectations held of him.

His role in the frame of the *Symposium*'s plot corresponds with this status. He is the man who has come too late, the man who has not been present from the start and who has not heard the most beautiful and the most elevated topic in the conversation, Diotima's 'initiation' into the nature of Eros. Even in real life this man had misunderstood Socrates' 'eroticism' and interpreted it as sexual interest (*Symposium* 217c–219d, esp. 218c).

It is an example of Plato's subtle dramatic irony when he selects none other than Alcibiades, who had once been tested by Socrates and was found to be too lightweight, and makes him characterise Socrates' nature. Certainly, he says much that is correct and important about him – things which are the result of his accurate recollection of what he had experienced. But when he tries to describe Socrates' logoi, it becomes evident how far off the mark he is from the true Socrates. For Alcibiades expresses the opinion that these logoi looked laughable at first sight, with their analogies to blacksmiths, shoemakers and tanners, except that one has to 'open' them to realise that only these logoi contain reason and the most divine images of virtue (*Symposium* 221d–222a).

It is obvious what type of Socratic logoi Alcibiades is referring to: the occasional conversations depicted in the early dialogues, which continually work with the analogy from *technê* and aim at drawing conclusions from the 'knowledge' of the 'artist' (the *technitês*) for the knowledge of the moral agent. The short exchange in the *Symposium* between Socrates and Agathon, which follows after Agathon's speech (199c–201c), also belongs to this type of elenctic and aporetic discussion. Alcibiades appears to know nothing else. But in the *Symposium* the elenctic discussion with Agathon is only the prelude for a résumé of quite different discussions, namely the repeated didactic philosophical discussions which Socrates had with Diotima and by means of which he received positive, uncoded instruction concerning Eros. Alcibiades, the man who has come too late, has no knowledge of discussions of such a kind. Hence the emphasis he lays on the shoemaker and tanner analogies and on the necessity to 'open' such dialogues. At the decisive moment Alcibiades himself was obviously not capable of 'opening' Socrates' words, which were imparted to him privately in an 'erotic' situation and which contain clear resonances of the idea of the gradation of the Beautiful in the speech of Diotima (*Symposium* 218d–219a); otherwise he would no longer have hoped for physical love (219b–c), nor would he have later drifted away from the unique teacher of 'virtue' (ἀρετή).

If we thus are correct in understanding Alcibiades' late arrival as a conscious and expressive dramaturgical decision of Plato's, we shall indeed see a correct and important interpretational maxim in the 'opening' of the dialogues (i.e. in the decipherment of hidden allusions). But we shall not overlook the fact that Plato introduces 'opening' very clearly as the interpretational method of those who know nothing of the more constructive philosophical logoi which lead higher up on the way to the *archai*. Alcibiades is not only our Platonic guarantor for 'opening'; he is also Plato's example for showing that 'opening' cannot be successful without explicit instruction on the decisive philosophical issues.

21

IRONY

Irony is perhaps Plato's most famous stylistic technique. The urbane lightness, elegance and nuancing of his ironic tone are without equal in the whole of world-literature, which is itself not lacking in irony, and are an inexhaustible source of delight for the educated reader.

There are many ways in which it can be applied: a whole direction of plot can be shaped by irony (as in the *Euthydemus*), a whole character can be revealed in the light of irony (like Euthyphro or Hippias); or the entrance of a character can be ironically qualified by the dramatic context (as we have just seen in the case of Alcibiades in the *Symposium*), or perhaps even only one single reaction of a character who is not otherwise subjected to irony (we may note for example Adeimantus' forgetfulness concerning the conditions which the discussion is subject to; *Republic* 504a–c).[90]

As versatile as Plato's use of irony may be,[91] it is none the less a method of presentation which is of limited range for him. It is of decisive importance that we do not confuse Platonic irony with the all-pervasive Romantic irony, which is a specifically modern phenomenon. Romantic irony is not directed towards a specific opponent, but against everything and anything; it penetrates the point of view of the ironist himself, in fact the ironist in particular; in essence, it is self-irony, and its most important function is to leave nothing, absolutely nothing, untouched which might escape ironic treatment. For the Romantic thinker there can be nothing absolute which might be immune from being relativised by irony. In the case of Plato, on the other hand, it is evident that irony stops short of what he calls the 'divine' realm of the eternally existent, and of the 'divine' *philosophia* as the attempt to grasp the realm of the eternally existent noetically. It is often remarked that the attitude in which Plato speaks of the realm of the Ideas has a clearly religious element.[92] For Plato, irony is only a means for producing this attitude in the reader as well, by revealing the falsity and risibility of opposing positions.

A sense of irony is thus without doubt important for reading Plato. At the same time we must guard against the error of making irony a central – and not merely a subsidiary – means of instruction in Plato. This view is found in the interpreters who on the one hand have seen that the aporetic dialogues on the virtues do not contain aporias about whose solution Plato could have been in any doubt, but who on the other hand have not been able to accept that Plato produces 'puzzles' which are unsolvable without recourse to other information – whether it be to his oral philosophy or to the doctrine of the virtues in the *Republic*; accordingly, it has been concluded, the ironic presentation must be sufficient unto itself for clarifying Plato's actual meaning. As promising as this thought might appear, when such interpretations are carried out it has been shown again and again that more is necessary for answering the open questions of the early works than merely the correction of the ironically sketched mistaken attitudes and mistaken judgments. One single example may suffice. In the *Hippias Minor* the thesis is 'proven' that the man who does wrong of his own free will is 'better' in comparison with the man who does so without free will. Socrates' discussion-partner, Hippias, who is treated with a great deal of biting irony, indeed disputes this false thesis but cannot counter Socrates' deliberately false argumentation with anything. But it would be quite pointless here to turn everything about Hippias that is presented ironically into its opposite if we do not know Socrates' thesis 'No one errs willingly'. If one has this thesis all the paradoxes of the *Hippias Minor* are resolved without difficulty. But in no passage of the dialogue can this thesis be recovered by simply cancelling out the irony. The reader must already be equipped with it if he wants to read with profit, or otherwise the dialogue will mean nothing to him. The 'ironic' interpreters of our times are equipped from the very beginning with the necessary knowledge by means of our cultural tradition; that is the only reason why they can imagine that they have extracted it from the dialogue 'without presuppositions'.[93]

It should have been realised all along that for Plato irony is a device of limited importance and function. The simple fact that it begins to recede markedly in important works of the middle period, makes only a marginal appearance in the major work, the *Republic*, and is almost entirely lacking in works like the *Timaeus* and the *Laws* should have safeguarded against the Romantic overestimation of irony's importance for Plato.

22

MYTH

In more than one respect, Plato's use of the 'mythical' style invites comparison with his use of irony: his myths are as famous as his uses of irony; they are likewise a source of ever new literary pleasure for the receptive reader; they are similarly versatile in terms of form and function; and, fourth, they have sometimes been just as overestimated.

On the one hand, Plato puts his myths in clear opposition to logos. On the other, it cannot be denied that, despite the clarity of the semantic opposition, he deliberately blurs the border between myth and logos in particular cases. We can see this even in the presentation of a myth told by someone other than Socrates: Protagoras, in the dialogue named after him, makes his audience choose between his presenting his point of view in the form of a myth or of a logos (*Protagoras* 320c); the choice is given back to him, at which he begins with the 'more pleasant' form, a myth. After speaking for some time he declares that he now no longer wants to offer myth but logos (324d6) – but at this point the alert reader has long since realised that the myth has turned into a logos considerably earlier (namely at 323a5, or, perhaps better, even earlier, at 322d5), without any sharp demarcation.

Plato does the same with his own myths. The story of the discovery of writing by Theuth (*Phaedrus* 274c–275b) has all the characteristics of a Platonic *mythos*: it takes place in distant primeval times, the agents are gods, and they are introduced with speaking roles; the subject of the story is a primeval divine 'discovery', i.e. the moment when the natural characteristics of a thing were determined once and for all. But Socrates has scarcely concluded his little story when Phaedrus remonstrates with him for inventing this Egyptian *logos*; so Phaedrus has wiped away the mythical elements of the story, and has recognised the logos in the myth in view of its

96

transparent message – a procedure which Socrates implicitly approves of by emphasising for his part that the only matter of importance is whether the facts referred to are presented accurately or not (275b–c).

In the same dialogue there is Socrates' great Eros-speech, whose core – the story of the ascent of the divine and human chariots of souls to the place beyond the heavens (246aff.) – depicts a story which is unambiguously mythical. The speech defines itself as 'proof' (ἀπόδειξις) of the thesis that Eros is given by the gods for the greatest happiness of the lover and the beloved – except that this proof would be incredible to the over-clever, but credible to the wise (245c1–2). This reference to the varied assessment and reception of what follows is not difficult to interpret: on the one hand, Plato reckons with readers who see only the mythical element of the story and thus decline to believe it, and at the same time he hopes for readers of the kind who understand that what is unproven by the myth not only needs proof but is also capable of being given it – a fact to which Plato in fact specifically refers[94] – and therefore accept the myth's message in view of the logos contained in it. The 'proof' of the thesis in any case begins with the proof of the immortality of the soul (245c5–246a2), which does not at all proceed by mythical narrative but in a strictly conceptual manner.

I have already remarked (pp. 68f.) that the mythical picture of the tripartite chariot of the soul is given justification in arguments of the fourth book of the *Republic*. Seen from the perspective of the myth in the *Phaedrus*, the *Republic* would thus have to be described as a logos; but we have already seen (p. 79) that Plato alludes to his major work with precisely the words 'in that he {sc. the philosopher} tells stories about justice' (δικαιοσύνης πέρι μυθολογοῦντα, *Phaedrus* 276e3). Of course, the *Republic*, as a utopian design which awaits realisation, also has a strongly mythical element: much is left to the creative imagination of its author and is unable to be measured against experience so far; but, above all, the 'mythical' character of the major work could be based on the fact that essential points, although in principle capable of substantiation, are not substantiated in fact.[95]

In this sense the whole essay of natural philosophy in the *Timaeus* is described as a 'probable myth' (29d, 68d, 69b), because here the ontological status of the subject rules out total substantiation or total certainty of substantiation.

In the greatest conceivable contrast with the *Timaeus*' philosophy of nature, which sometimes operates with new, extremely difficult concepts, there are the myths of the other world, which, in the manner of traditional religious stories, depict the lot of the just and the unjust after death. Even here Plato plays with the opposition between myth and logos, as when he makes Socrates say when introducing the myth in the *Gorgias* that what he is about to produce will be something which Callicles indeed will regard as a myth, but for himself it is a logos, because it is true (*Gorgias* 523a). Certainly we must not understand this as if Plato were declaring the truth of the story that under Cronos and at the beginning of the supremacy of Zeus judgment was passed on a mortal's life on his last day on this side of the grave, and, what is more, by judges who for their part still lived in this life (523b–524a). None the less, for Plato the truth of belief in immortality and the conviction that our future fate in the afterlife depends on our ethical conduct in this life remains an unshakeable reality. But because Callicles knows nothing of the internal structure of the soul (see above, p. 69f.) and consequently does not know the philosophical concept of justice either (alluded to by Socrates at 526c3–4), which is derived from the structure of the soul, he cannot understand the logos in the myth, for which reason he will discard it as a 'mere' myth. The varying assessments of the myth of the hereafter as a logos by Socrates and as a myth by Callicles are in perfect accord with the expected double evaluation of the Eros-speech in the *Phaedrus*, about which we have just spoken (above, p. 97).[96]

It is against this background that we should consider the much-discussed question of whether myth in Plato is subordinate to logos or whether it imparts a higher truth which cannot be reached by logos.

The second assumption, that the myths have a greater capacity for truth, derives from the perception of modern irrationalist trends and cannot be supported by any arguments of Plato's. On the other hand, subordinating myth under logos cannot be accepted either, if by that one means that myth is a more or less dispensable decoration, a merely illustrative way of putting insights which can be achieved in other ways. Had this been Plato's view of the role of myth, he would hardly have been able to devote such space to it in his writings. To be sure, the dialectic exploration of reality, which is achieved in argumentational logos, is the ultimate aim of the philosopher. By the same token, he cannot dispense with the entertainment-value of myth; moreover, the ability of pictures and stories to depict a fact in its entirety and intuitively is an indispensable supplement to conceptual analysis. Looked at in this way, myth proves itself to be a second approach to reality which indeed cannot be independent of logos in terms of content, but represents an advantage compared with it which cannot be replaced by anything else.[97]

23

MONOLOGUE AND DIALOGUE
WITH IMAGINARY PARTNERS

The myths are presented in continuous speech. They provide the most visible evidence that the discussion-leader can leave dialogue behind and use a *makros logos*. The longest and philosophically most important two of these mythical monologues, the lecture of Timaeus and Socrates' great speech on Eros in the *Phaedrus*, mostly contain things which in traditional thinking would no longer be categorised as 'mythical' – the conversation-leader has thus given up the communicational mode of dialogue under the name of myth, and has made the transition to instructing in monologue-form.

Another means of leaving dialogue behind is dialogue within the dialogue. Here I am not thinking of the literary technique of the framework-dialogue, as it can be seen used in the *Phaedo* and the *Euthydemus* among other dialogues, but of the way in which the conversation which has been held till now is temporarily interrupted by the conversation-leader and by the introduction of an imaginary person, whether as an imagined possibility or as a report of a conversation which has allegedly been held in the past. Indeed, formally it might look merely as if another conversation-partner is being included, as happens repeatedly in the Platonic dialogues. But because the new 'person' is clearly differentiated from the persons present at the conversation in that he does not have any individuality of his own but is simply representative of a certain position or a certain mentality, he can easily be recognised as a construction of the conversation-leader, who thus preserves the dialogue-form by means of the device while in reality suspending the conversation actually held up to this point in order to be able to give it the direction he desires.

To this day, this literary device of Plato's has nowhere been described, although Plato frequently has recourse to it and although its significance for understanding the dialogue-form is considerable.

Diotima is the most famous of the imaginary partner-substitutes. Of course, there may have once been a seeress in Mantinea (several archaeologists even identify a marble head of the fourth century as a portrait of Diotima); but Socrates' conversations with Diotima are clearly conceived as a continuation of the conversation which Socrates has been holding with his real partner, Agathon (see *Symposium* 201e). In that Socrates now takes over the role held till now by Agathon, the conversation can be raised to heights which would have been incredible with Agathon as partner. Socrates indeed delivers his contribution to the praise of Eros in terms of a dialogue (though only until 208b – from there on Diotima speaks in monologue), but in reality on his own, as other participants in the group have done.

Important points of view and conclusions are arrived at by means of an anonymous third party in the tenth book of the *Laws* where the Athenian anticipates the answers and reactions of atheists in the future in order to provide pre-emptive philosophical defence for the law against impiety (893aff.), or in the *Protagoras*, where Socrates informs anonymous representatives of the actual meaning of their hedonism (*Protagoras* 353aff.). Most clearly conceived as a mask of the dialectician, however, is the anonymous third person in the *Hippias Maior*, who even lives in Socrates' house and shows him, after his return 'home' (*Hippias Maior* 304d4), the way to a more adequate treatment of the problems than is possible with Hippias. Finally, in the *Phaedo* Socrates informs us in a long 'quotation' (66b3–67b2) what the 'people who truly conduct philosophical inquiry' would say to one another (πρὸς ἀλλήλους) about the search for truth and about the relationship between body and soul.

The philosophical meaning of the literary technique of the imaginary dialogue within a dialogue appears to be a double one. The fact that even what the dialectician offers from the wealth of his own insights without the participation of the real conversation-partner is presented in the form of a dialogue means that thinking, as a conversation of the soul with itself, is in a fundamental sense dialogical. Thinking which aims for a validity which is recognised interpersonally must in principle satisfy the requirement that it expose itself to criticism by its opponent and stand up to it. Thus Plato shows that even the dialectician's conclusions, which have been achieved in lonely cogitation 'at home', are conclusions resulting from communal investigation. Second, we can also gather from this that the Platonic dialectician, even though his thinking necessarily does satisfy the *a priori* requirement of interpersonal (dialogical) examinability, is in fact at no time required to depend on a particular partner and a particular situation in order to come to a particular conclusion. Rather, he brings the decisive insights ready-made to the discussion; at his discretion, he can develop them even without the real partner by bringing them forth as the result of earlier agreements reached with an imaginary partner. But he can also, if it seems right to him, remain silent about them (see *Phaedrus* 276a6–7).

24

THE CHARACTERISTICS OF
THE DIALOGUES
What they really mean

We have now collected sufficient examples for us to return to our list of the essential characteristics of the Platonic dialogues and to be able to inquire into their original meaning. The critique of writing in the *Phaedrus* provides the essential points of view for interpreting the form of the dialogues. Only this clue *of Plato's own* can give us the guarantee that we are not privileging modern habits of thought and prejudices over Plato's own intentions.

We shall now consider, in reverse order, the characteristics enumerated above (p. 18f.).

(7) We must start from the basic insight that no writing, and therefore no Platonic dialogue, is in the position to bring itself the necessary support in the case of attack. The dialectician or *philosophos* is, on the other hand, distinguished precisely by his ability to support his writings orally; in this way he will reveal 'things of greater value' (*timiôtera*) and thereby prove his writings to be (comparatively) negligible. Now if Plato's dialogues are the writings of a *philosophos* (and this supposition can scarcely be doubted), a fund of philosophical *timiôtera* must exist behind them which could in principle be communicated in writing but which the author deliberately does not commit to writing. The existence of an oral philosophy behind the dialogues is thus above all a *deduction* which results conclusively from the application of the critique of writing to Plato's own written works. But it is secondarily directly confirmed in a striking way by the 'gaps'. Interpreted in the light of the critique of writing, the 'gaps' convey a very clear message; through them Plato says nothing other than 'This written work is the writing of a *philosophos* who can substantiate what he has explained here more precisely by means of the spoken word with insights and theories, in comparison with which the present written work would appear less important.'

(6) The basic situation depicted in the dialogues is always the βοήθεια-situation. It is a method of testing whether someone is a *philosophos* or not. Whenever a thesis is expressed it is attacked: its originator must show that he can defend it with arguments which reach more deeply. Only one figure is ever capable of this qualitative raising of the level of argumentation, which is so typical of the structure of the dialogues: the figure, always the same, of the Platonic dialectician. Passing the philosopher's test is not simply a question of intelligence (otherwise Protagoras and Gorgias would be able to support their logos), but is bound up with the knowledge of the Ideas and Platonic dialectic.

(5) Now it also becomes comprehensible why the dialectician always proves himself to be invincible and is not reduced to the level of the lesser stature of the conversation-partners even by minor defeats or occasional mistakes. He tests the others in front of the background of his *timiôtera*; he is the 'man with knowledge' (the εἰδώς, *Phaedrus* 276a, 278c) who has attained the knowledge of the Ideas; opposite him the others, inasmuch as they lack the philosophy of Ideas, are basically 'learners' (μανθάνοντες; see *Phaedrus* 276a5). The dialogues again and again show the same situation: the dialectician's search for the 'appropriate soul' (see *Phaedrus* 276e6).

The dialectician's invincibility, which has irritated many readers, is in any case not only to be seen in the actual progress of the conversations but is also expressed directly: Socrates, says Alcibiades, would conquer *everyone*, and indeed *always* (*Symposium* 214e3–4); and for the recognition of the Good, says Socrates in the *Republic*, the dialectician must have passed all attempts at refutation without being harmed (534c1–3). Thus here too we see that Plato's theoretical picture of the philosopher is in full agreement with the literary portrait of the dialectician in the dialogues.

(4) The dialectician's basic superiority is also the cause of his always being shown in conversation with only one partner.[98] The discussion-leader has the authority to enforce concentration on one theme with one partner. Considering several points of view simultaneously and on a par would only distract from the fundamental difference between the person who already has the 'turning of the soul' (περιαγωγὴ τῆς ψυχῆς, *Republic* 521c6; cf. 518c8–d4) by means of the philosophy of the Ideas behind him and the person who still has it in front of him. The philosophical distance from the dialectician must become repeatedly clear step by step, with each partner, not to humiliate him but to prepare him for the possible transition. Other points of view than that of the philosophy of Ideas

cannot be made fruitful even in debate with one another; thus there are no moments in the conversation in which the dialectician would withdraw and temporarily leave the discussion to others (Hippias' attempt at *Protagoras* 347a–b to introduce his own logos into the discussion as a third alongside those of Protagoras and Socrates shows clearly that Plato did not avoid this possibility by chance but on purpose: Hippias is rejected).

If the dialectician enters a discussion which has been started by others, as Socrates does in the *Cratylus*, it is he (not the opponents up to this point) who brings the views of both sides into relation with one another, in order, finally, to measure them both against his own position. One must not measure falsity against falsity; rather, 'true philosophy' is the measure for all differing opinions. But since all humans have a vague memory of what their soul once saw in its incorporeal state and of which only the philosopher of the Ideas possesses a clearer memory, they are driven by a longing, however unconscious, for the knowledge of the dialectician. In the final analysis, therefore, it is the partner who needs conversation with the dialectician and not the reverse. The plot of the dialogues shows this again and again, even if with varying degrees of clarity. I refer to the *Laches* and *Charmides*, where the appropriate teacher is sought for; or the *Symposium*, where Socrates changes from being the courting lover into the courted beloved; but particularly the plot of the *Republic* which revolves solely around the others' not wanting to let the dialectician 'get away',[99] because they could not make any progress with the questions which concern them without his insights. For his part, the dialectician is never dependent on a particular partner, and he even clearly demonstrates this: he can suspend the conversation and direct it wherever he wants with the help of an imaginary 'partner'.

(3) Thus the dialogues have a sovereign discussion-*leader*. Indeed, Plato's masterly art of presentation can often create the impression that Socrates subordinates himself with perfect politeness to the ideas which the partner has of the conversation. But that is clearly only an appearance preserved for the sake of urbanity; more precise observation can always show that the dialectician has the strings of the conversation in his hands. In the *Protagoras* he subjects the famous sophist to his method of short questions and answers (in the dispute over methods; 334c–338e); in the *Republic* he himself defines how far his friends may press and 'compel' him. Finally, the question of 'command' in the conversation is also openly expressed: when Socrates reproaches Meno for 'commanding', the obvious irony

there is a clear hint that this privilege can only be bestowed on him.[100]

There is no conversation among equals in Plato. The only time that he makes men of equal intellectual capacity come together,[101] in the *Timaeus*, he avoids dialogue: Timaeus delivers a monologue of several hours' duration before Socrates, Critias and Hermogenes. Describing a conversation among several perfect dialecticians would actually have to have been the most rewarding task of all for an author with Plato's literary talent. The lack of such a conversation is a puzzle for those interpreters who assume that Plato wanted to entrust his thinking in its full range to writing and to this end created the dialogue as a self-sufficient form of writing. But the puzzle is solved without difficulty if we take the critique of writing as our measure: a discussion among intellectually equal dialecticians would immediately have to rise into those regions of the theory of principles which the philosopher deliberately reserves for *oral* defence. For example, if Timaeus had to support his 'myth' under the critical questioning of Socrates, he would have to reveal those 'even higher principles' which he so carefully keeps out of his discourse (53d), or he would have to expose the nature of the Demiurge which however, according to *Timaeus* 28c, cannot be imparted 'to everyone', i.e. in writing. That is why the *Timaeus* is the only dialogue without a discussion-leader: *these* listeners do not need any 'leading'. But it is also the only dialogue without discussion: the dialectic exchange of such participants in the conversation would no longer be 'for everyone'.

(2) If we compare the exceptional dialogue, the *Timaeus*, with the remaining works it becomes evident that it also lacks the usual lively description of the place and the time of the encounter and of the individual character of the participants. This cannot be by chance: in the *Phaedo* Socrates, as is well known, says that one should leave one's person out of account and pay attention to the truth only (91c). The ability to do that is indeed something which can only be achieved by long practice; the way the *Phaedo* continues shows clearly enough that the listeners present were not in a position to do that. The audience of Timaeus' lecture are in that respect on a higher level: Plato lets us know scarcely anything about their individual personalities, and what he does impart has no influence on the progress of the discussion.

Leaving one's individuality out of account is thus a task for the 'learner'. The task for the dialectician lies elsewhere: in his search for appropriate partners he could hardly leave out of account *their* individual requirements and peculiarities, which make it difficult for them – and for each of them in different ways – to enter into philosophical inquiry in any other manner. The aim of a philosophically based 'rhetoric' is to offer each soul the 'speeches' which suit it (*Phaedrus* 277b–c). The dialogues illustrate the dialectician's ability in this.

The characters introduced are without exception 'colourful' souls (see *Phaedrus* 277c2), i.e. unstable souls, not yet sufficiently purified in philosophical terms. If the dialectician seeks the right logoi for each of them, this means that he is not operating in the region which is his aim – in the region of purely conceptual knowledge (see *Republic* 511b–c) which leads upwards to the principle and back from it to the multiplicity of the Ideas.

The strong emphasis on the unique and the individual in the dialogues thus reminds us not only that we must each devote ourselves to the 'true philosophy' personally, as characters with some limitation or other, but also that exclusively individual characteristics are something which philosophy will help to overcome in favour of a depersonalised, objective search after the truth which is orientated purely by the ὄντα (by reality), and third that in his writings Plato wanted to depict only those phases which *precede* this strict dialectical search for the truth, while the dialectical search for truth itself necessarily remains reserved for oral philosophical inquiry.

(1) In the light of all this, the fact that Plato depicts *conversations* does not mean either that philosophical insights are to be won only in the company of others (the dialectician can often make greater progress in company with imaginary figures, i.e. in his own company),[102] or that dialogue is the only legitimate form of imparting philosophical knowledge and insights (Timaeus can help himself to a continuing sequence of arguments). Being in dialogue, as a way of living, is not decisive either, for meeting over philosophy over a long period, indeed living together, which the Seventh Letter speaks about (συνουσία, συζῆν, 341c6, 7), is precisely what cannot be depicted in the dialogues. In contrast with modern views which emphasise only the process of holding dialogue as such, Plato was concerned with depicting the agreement (homology) which is reached in dialogue. The presence of the superior figure of the dialectician, who knows the 'truth' about his subject, lends its weight to the homology which is acquired in company. Even if the final proof is lacking, whatever agreement is reached under the leadership of Socrates, the Stranger from Elea or

the Athenian is not the empty chatter of people who commit themselves today to this and tomorrow to that, without responsibility with regard to the truth. What Plato wants to create is a homology *which can be accounted for*. The result which the dialectician attains with his partners is a result which rational human beings *should* agree upon. Plato is so far removed from hiding behind the views and opinions of his figures, and from thus being 'anonymous', that he untiringly depicts the *correct* homology, by which the reader *should* orient himself. The way Plato marks what is correct as correct by directing plot and manipulating sympathy can, as in the *Gorgias* or the *Phaedo* for example, reach a degree of unambiguity which leaves nothing to be desired. Continuing to speak here of 'indirect communication' could still formally be defensible, but in fact it would be singularly misleading. Plato does not use the possibilities of the genre of drama to produce maximal ambivalence,[103] but as a rule he leads the reader by means of frequently ambivalent steps to a clear final result[104] and to the equally clear assurance that further substantiation and tracing back to 'even higher principles' is as yet forthcoming, but is necessary and possible.

25

HOW AND WHY THE DIALOGUE-FORM HAS BEEN MISUNDERSTOOD

We can now say, when we look back at the modern theory of the Platonic dialogues (see pp. 28–32 esp. 29) which ascribes to the written dialogues the task which Plato reserves for spoken philosophical inquiry, that this theory is not only unPlatonic in the sense that it has no Platonic text to support it (see above, p. 30), but also anti-Platonic in the sense that it contravenes the spirit and letter of the critique of writing and deliberately turns a deaf ear to Plato's continual and clear references to his oral doctrine of principles.

The modern theory of the dialogues attempts a rehabilitation of writing in the face of Plato's own critique of it, and in the final analysis it attempts an equation of writing and orality in the decisive matter of how the philosopher's 'more valuable things' (*timiôtera*) are imparted.

But the rehabilitation of the written dialogues is only achieved by a series of metaphors. The fact that a dialogue might itself 'select' its reader does not mean the same as when Plato says of the dialectician that he selects for himself an 'appropriate soul' (λαβὼν ψυχὴν προσήκουσαν, *Phaedrus* 276e6): this certainly means an active choice, but in the case of the dialogue-book 'selecting' only means that many a reader puts it aside in boredom while many another does not. But that does not make for a special case of the dialogues (it is also true of stock market reports). Or, if an inappropriate person still reads the dialogue, the dialogue 'is silent' by 'hiding' its deeper level – a mere metaphor for the simple fact that not every reader understands all the references of the meaning; consequently, the dialogue's 'answering' and the 'support' which it is supposed to be able to bring itself is only a metaphor for the ability of the reader's comprehension to grow with time. But that too is perfectly true of other forms of the use of writing.

By the selection of a partner, by the possibility of pausing and being silent, by 'support', Plato does not mean things which passively happen to the philosopher's logos when it is considered by its readership, but modes of behaviour by which the dialectician actively directs the conversation. Thus we can rule out the possibility that what Plato had in mind was a metaphorical reinterpretation when applied to the written dialogue. For Plato, it would not have been sensible to attempt to rehabilitate any specific type of the use of writing (e.g. his own dialogues), in view of the general aim of the critique of writing. In opposition to writing, which he confronts in quite general terms, he places oral philosophical inquiry, but not dialogue in book-form, which is alleged to have a privileged position: *no* book can store new answers to new questions since the text is now firmly established and 'always says one and the same thing only' (*Phaedrus* 275d9).

The special status assigned to the dialogues does not merely lack any support in *Plato*'s reflections on putting writing to philosophical use, but over and above that is also extremely dubious *when looked at objectively*. According to the modern theory, the dialogues alone should be exempted from the verdict of the critique of writing. But, once the metaphorical interpretation is admitted, it soon becomes apparent that many other forms of written exposition 'by themselves choose their readers for themselves', because they 'are silent' to inappropriate readers, and that they 'do not always say the same thing' in answer to questions. Who would want to deny these (metaphorical) capabilities to the lyric poetry of Hölderlin, the novels of Dostoevsky or Umberto Eco, the pastoral novel of Longus, the dramas of Euripides or even the profound historical work of Herodotus?[105] We should mention Theognis and Pindar here as well, for they clearly state that their verse contains the right message only for those who are qualified for it.[106] All authors who produce such 'active' writings would suddenly have to become philosophers, if the metaphorical reinterpretation were legitimate, and the whole critique of writing would lose its critical meaning, since there would be more exceptions than cases which fit the rule.

Without doubt Plato too hoped for the 'right' reader – but that is something that other poets and writers, whom Plato would not have regarded as worthy of the name of *philosophos*, did as well. And Plato also unquestionably made use of 'indirect communication' and gave much information only by means of allusions; but by doing so he also took his place in the circle of the non-philosophical authors. But the critique of writing says unmistakably that the *philosophos* is distinguished from other authors precisely by means of his relationship to writing. As a *philosophos*, Plato departs from usual practice by consciously not entrusting everything to writing, not even in a coded form, but reserves for oral exposition the 'things of greater value' in his theory of principles as a support for his works. However, the techniques of 'indirect communication' remain for him merely a subsidiary means of philosophical communication, which is basically not suited to replace oral esotericism since by means of it the 'clarity and certainty' of knowledge which the philosopher attains in dialectical discussion is not attainable.

To return to Ludwig Wittgenstein's expressive metaphor in the *Vermischte Bemerkungen* (see p. 28f.): Plato did not reject hanging in front of the 'doors' of his 'rooms' 'locks' which were to catch the eye of certain readers only and could be opened by them alone. But this form of protection, which was and is standard from Theognis to Wittgenstein and beyond, was not sufficient for him: besides the 'locks' he put up signs, easily visible for all, which say without secretiveness and 'deeper meaning' that apart from the 'rooms' of the dialogues there are further rooms which will be reached only by those who are prepared to submit themselves to the effort of the 'longer way' of oral dialectic.

One must finally ask how these misinterpretations, which are now gradually giving way to a new image of Plato, ever came into being.

One conducive factor was the understandable and widespread, but ultimately naive, tendency to align the great thinkers of the past with the attitudes of one's own times. Because the victory of unrestricted openness in the imparting of knowledge has become irreversible for the modern period since the Enlightenment and because esotericism is thus no longer a possible option, readers have wanted to rediscover the new attitude in Plato as well. Against this background we have an explanation for the universal inability of the nineteenth and twentieth centuries to take the critique of writing seriously and to apply it to the dialogues themselves.

More particularly, the misunderstandings have been nourished by long-lived prejudices about the opposing position: taking Plato's doctrine of principles into account would lead, people have thought, to a 'devaluation' of the dialogues or to a 'dogmatic' Plato or to 'secret teachings'. But the 'devaluation', as we have seen, comes from Plato himself and cannot be shared by us anyway, since we cannot possess the oral philosophy in its original form. Why Plato is supposed to have been more dogmatic in his oral discussion of the principles than for example in his doctrine of the soul, as we possess it in the dialogues, is incomprehensible. We need not fear any secret teachings: Plato did not consider his thinking on the principles as secret (ἀπόρρητα), but as 'not prematurely communicable' (ἀπρόρρητα; see p. 62). Since the usual prejudices have hindered the understanding of this Platonic distinction, I shall attempt to clarify them here in a little more detail.

26

THE DIFFERENCE BETWEEN ESOTERICISM AND SECRECY

Plato's activity as a philosophical writer cannot be fully understood as long as the distinction between esotericism and secrecy is not understood. The distinction becomes clear by means of a comparison between the Seventh Letter, handed down to us under Plato's name, and the Pythagorean tradition on the profanisation of certain doctrines of the community.

Aristotle and Aristoxenus attest to the fact that secrecy was typical of the early Pythagoreans.[107] The story was later told that a member of the community, Hippasus (or Hipparchus) by name, was the first to break the silence and make a mathematical discovery of Pythagoras' accessible to all. The reaction of the community was to banish Hippasus and to erect a grave for him: for the other Pythagoreans he was henceforth 'dead'. But as a punishment for his crime a deity had him drowned in the sea.[108]

Whether or not the story has a core of truth, it shows in any case what secrecy means. The deity, it says, imposed a just punishment: that can only mean that the Pythagoreans bound themselves by an oath not to make their communal knowledge public (without a religious tie the gods need not have intervened). The banishment of the rebel by declaring him dead must have been an effective sanction as long as the political strength of the community was unbroken. The motive for the banishment was scarcely concern about the appropriate reception of the material to be withheld: it was a matter of a mathematical theorem, and thus of a type of material which can most readily be passed on without taking account of the inner makeup of the recipient. Obviously, the real issue was the privilege of knowledge. It is therefore not surprising that Hippasus was later ascribed democratic sympathies:[109] anyone who makes any knowledge public which privileges a community is obviously regarded as the subverter of the strength of the community in other respects as well.

Let us compare this with the attitude which can be observed in the Seventh Letter. (Whether this letter is genuine or not is of as little consequence in this context as the possible historical kernel of the story of Hippasus: what matters here is only the difference between two basic attitudes which are often wrongly confused.)

Dionysius is not reproached for breaking any oath. Nor does Plato call down the gods' punishment on him; indeed, he does not even think of outlawing any memory of him in the circle of his philosophical and political friends in the Academy and in Syracuse; instead, he even has positive things to say about Dionysius and refuses to support the war against him (338d6, 340a, 350c–d). One reprimand remains, however, and it is a weighty one: Dionysius has brought himself to circulate in book-form what he had heard from Plato during private instruction about the ultimate aims of his philosophical inquiry. His motive can only have been 'ugly ambition' (344e2). In contrast with Plato himself (344d7) Dionysius felt no respect for the matters discussed and did not stop at disseminating things which can only be successfully understood after a long philosophical preparation and which once formulated are exposed in the highest degree to the danger of misunderstanding and distortion by unphilosophical or even ill-disposed recipients. Thus Plato is not concerned about the strength and influence of the Academy; however, what hurts him is the misjudgment of what matters to him philosophically, and the possibility that things might be debased whose objective value he is deeply convinced of. His reaction to Dionysius' publishing fragments of his oral philosophy is not moral outrage but unutterable human disappointment.

The contrast between the two basic attitudes now becomes clearly comprehensible: *secrecy* is based on compulsion. Anyone who breaks it breaks his oath and exposes himself to the sanctions of his former group. Secrecy means keeping any knowledge which privileges the group in the group's possession in order to maintain its strength: knowledge kept in secret is thus a means to an end.

Esotericism is a requirement of reason, not the result of compulsion by a group. Anyone who trespasses against esoteric reserve is not exposing himself to any sanctions at all; he is thereby not harming the community but the cause in question: thinking about the principles, a process rich in preconditions, cannot develop its positive effect if it is received in the wrong way through lack of adequate preparation. Philosophical knowledge is not a means to an end but an end in itself, and should therefore be passed on properly, with necessary circumspection, not promulgated mechanically. In short, esotericism is directed to a cause, secrecy to power.

Seen from the perspective of the twentieth century, this distinction might in spite of everything seem unimportant: one could insist that the only relevant thing is that in the case of both basic attitudes knowledge is still imparted restrictively. The answer to that is that the one-sided point of view of the twentieth century cannot be binding for the evaluation of Plato. Our modern conviction that it is desirable that all research and all knowledge meet with unrestricted circulation is a historically recent phenomenon: it finally prevailed only in the seventeenth century and in the subsequent period of the Enlightenment and belief in progress. The Seventh Letter, however, considers that it is inappropriate to disseminate Plato's oral philosophy to everybody indiscriminately (341e1–2). The agreement with the view of the critique of writing (*Phaedrus* 275e1–3) is clear. It would be quite unhistorical to insinuate that Plato would accept the modern preference for disseminating knowledge on principle. If this view is ruled out, however, the difference between the two types of 'restrictive' knowledge-dissemination becomes all the more important. Moreover, if one considers the importance which free and rational decisions have in Plato's thought, one will not hesitate to attach fundamental importance to the difference between esotericism and secrecy as well.

27

PLATO'S CONCEPT OF PHILOSOPHY AND THE OBJECTIVES OF THE DIALOGUES

The trend to assimilate Plato to modern habits of thought at any price has not stopped at his concept of philosophy. Not a few interpreters have wanted to rediscover in his writings the infinitivism of German Romanticism. According to this interpretation, Plato thought that philosophy was a journey of thought without end, a perpetual striving and searching which indeed never reaches a final goal; the philosopher has nothing to present that he would not immediately question; philosophical propositions are consequently always temporary propositions, philosophical truth always truth to be retrieved.

Today we know, especially as a result of the systematic and historical works of Hans Krämer and Karl Albert, that this idea in no way corresponds with Plato's concept of philosophy.[110]

Throughout his work, Plato presents dialectic not as a utopian, unreal vision of another, superhuman mode of gaining knowledge, but as a real possibility, a walkable path which leads to an attainable goal. Once the soul has arrived at this goal and the 'end of its wandering', it finds rest from the effort of the search (see *Republic* 532e). This goal is the Idea of the Good, which is knowable for the human *nous*, just as its analogue in the realm of the senses, the sun, can be seen by the human eye (*Republic* 516b, 517b–c). God can recognise the principles, as can the human being who stands near him, i.e. the philosopher (*Timaeus* 53d). Thus it is in the recognition of the principles and the Ideas that the 'approximation to God' occurs which is at the same time the ontological and ethical aim of human beings (see *Republic* 500c, 613b, *Theaetetus* 176b, *Phaedrus* 253b, *Timaeus* 90d, *Laws* 716c). The knowledge of the Ideas is an enduring knowledge, ἐπιστήμη, and ἐπιστήμη 'binds tight' what is correct with reasons, makes it lasting (*Meno* 98d), and thus preserves it from being continuously questioned and formulated anew. However, approximation to God does not dissolve the ontological difference between God and human. The difference does not consist of man's not attaining the definitive knowledge of the Ideas and the principle – *Symposium* 210e, *Phaedrus* 249c and *Phaedo* 107b also talk of reaching the goal – but of man's ability to remain only temporarily in the knowledge which defines the nature of God, and in his repeated sinking back into a preoccupation with inessentials. For that reason, Eros embodies the essence of philosophy: Eros indeed reaches what he strives for, but what he reaches escapes him again (*Symposium* 203e).[111]

Philosophical talk is always exposed to the danger of misunderstanding; the dialogues give examples of that again and again. As a matter of fact, the knowledge of the Ideas cannot be enforced. The objects of knowledge are very dissimilar: the incorporeal as the 'most beautiful and most important' is indeed of a higher ontological level, but harder to know (*Politicus* 285d10–286b2). Similarly, within this realm there are differences of levels (*Republic* 485b6), which means, according to the simile of the cave, that the difficulty of the knowledge reaches its extreme point with ontological nearness to the Idea of the Good (*Republic* 515c4–517b7). And the nearer thinking comes to the difficult knowledge of the principles the less one can depend on imparting it unimpededly. Writing absolutely never reaches the degree of 'clarity and certainty' of knowledge which is imperative for the dialectician precisely in the realm of the *archai*.

The conclusion which Plato drew from this is that the philosopher does well not to entrust his thinking in all its range to writing. His motive for this reserve is his responsibility for the cause of the 'divine' philosophy. Since Plato appeals to the reason of the writer (*Phaedrus* 276b–c; cf. *Letter* 7, 343a, 344c–d), he thinks of a free decision: thus in principle what is withheld is communicable, even in writing. Looked at in terms of its content it is the 'more worthwhile thing', i.e. substantiation from the 'even higher principles'.

Accordingly, the dialogues are not going to be the complete presentation of Plato's entire philosophy. They do not even reveal the latest state of his thinking at each point. But what they reveal is something infinitely valuable: they reveal paths into philosophy which can be sought out and and trodden by individual people, afflicted with mistakes and limitations like ours. By means of their vivid liveliness the dialogues reveal an incomparable protreptic power, i.e. a power which turns us to philosophy. But the protreptic element is not all: we experience not only a longing for and an embarcation upon philosophy but also important steps on the path of philosophy towards the principles. The protreptic element cannot be separated from the discussion of important things, since it is precisely the very weight of the 'more worthwhile things' which has the strongest protreptic effect. Thus they must be revealed somehow, even if under the limitations which the critique of writing imposes on the philosopher's use of writing.

Thus the dialogues are to be read as fragments of Plato's philosophy with a propensity to encourage the reader and at the same time to point beyond themselves. But the form must be regarded as essential for the content. The dialogues are thus to be read as *dramas*: as plays with a continuous plot and a carefully thought-out constellation of characters. Again and again the plot shows that philosophical instruction is not randomly available, ready like wares for any purchaser, but is imparted only in accordance with the intellectual and moral maturity of the recipient; the plot shows, second, that, for raising the level of argumentation in the sequence of 'cases of support', and thus for passing the philosophers' test, only one figure is competent, namely the representative of the philosophy of Ideas. The upshot of this is the unchanging but never boring constellation of characters: the dialectician as a man with a philosophical advantage which cannot be caught up with stands in opposition to people who can be very ungifted or very gifted, but who in every case are still undeveloped, still insufficiently advanced. In view of this inequality the dialectician must make himself the leader in the conversation; he leads the partners to homologies (agreements) which are appropriate to their state of knowledge. The unambiguity of the constellation of characters guarantees that the homologies arrived at are not random and irrelevant but exemplary – i.e. the best that can be attained in these defined conditions. Thus what finally appears, after all kinds of detours, to be consolidated by agreement must be taken seriously as information which is meant by the author to be valid. But the 'gaps' must also be taken seriously; they do not have the standing of asides, but are introduced into the development of the plot as defining its structure: they draw attention to the fact that the discussion-leader could lead us to yet other, more deeply founded homologies.

Thus, by means of their consistently sustained literary technique, the dialogues refer to Plato's oral philosophy. In this way they prove themselves to be works of a *philosophos* in the sense defined in the critique of writing.

NOTES

1 On this passage see further below, p. 69f.
2 See my interpretation of the dialogue in *Platon und die Schriftlichkeit der Philosophie. Interpretationen zu den frühen und mittleren Dialogen* (Berlin and New York 1985) 191–207, esp. 197f. (This book will be cited hereafter as *PSP*.)
3 R.K. Merton, *The Sociology of Science* (Chicago and London 1973) esp. 273ff.
4 See *Cratylus* 383b–384a, 427d–e; *Euthyphro* 3d, 11b, 14c, 15e; *Protagoras* 341d; *Charmides* 174b; *Gorgias* 499b–c; *Hippias Minor* 370e, 373b; *Hippias Maior* 300c–d; *Ion* 541e.
5 For a more detailed argument for this interpretation of the *Euthydemus* see my 'Sokrates' Spott über Geheimhaltung. Zum Bild des φιλόσοφος in Platons *Euthydemos*', *Antike und Abendland* 26 (1980) 75–89, together with the chapter on Euthydemus in *PSP* (above, n. 2) 49–65.
6 Almost every dialogue contains something relevant to this theme. I have tried to give a comprehensive picture of the Socratic manner of imparting philosophical insights in *PSP*.
7 For the treatment of the 'gaps' in scholarship see *PSP* 324f. with n. 144. The first scholar to have recognised the significance of these passages clearly was Hans Joachim Krämer, *Arete bei Platon und Aristoteles* (Heidelberg 1959) 389ff.
8 It is quite a separate matter that it does indeed depend on the reactions of each individual partner *how much* of his views and insights Socrates imparts to him: see p. 69ff.
9 *Symposium* 175b, 220c–d; *Crito* 49a; *Meno* 81a; *Gorgias* 493a; *Hippias Maior* 304d; *Republic* 505a3, 611b9–10; *Phaedo* 100b5.
10 *Theaetetus* 189e, *Sophist* 263e.
11 *Protagoras* 348d.
12 An early example is Heinrich von Stein, *Sieben Bücher zur Geschichte des Platonismus* (Göttingen 1862) vol. 1, 11f.; more recently Ludwig Edelstein, 'Platonic Anonymity', *American Journal of Philology* 83 (1962) 1–22 has been influential.
13 In *PSP* I tried to repair this omission in research on Plato since Schleiermacher (who paved the way for this mode of interpretation).

120

NOTES

14 See Reinhold Merkelbach, *Platons Menon* (Frankfurt a.M. 1988), Introduction 5–10; Michael Erler, *Der Sinn der Aporien in den Dialogen Platons* (Berlin and New York 1987).
15 Perhaps with the sole exception of the second part of the *Parmenides*.
16 See Merkelbach, *Platons Menon* 6.
17 Ludwig Wittgenstein, *Vermischte Bemerkungen: Eine Auswahl aus dem Nachlaß, edited by Georg Henrik von Wright, with the collaboration of Heikki Nyman (Frankfurt a.M. 1977) 23.*
18 In the formulation of Paul Friedländer, *Platon* I³ (1964) 177, 'The dialogue is the only book-form which appears to overcome the book itself.'
19 In the 'Introduction' to his translation of Plato (vol. I, 1 (Berlin 1804) 5–36).
20 See the quotation, p. 28f.
21 See also p. 110 with n. 106.
22 Xenophanes *DK* 21 B 10 (*DK* = Diels–Kranz, *Die Fragmente der Vorsokratiker*, I, 1952⁶, 131).
23 Xenophanes *DK* 21 B 15 and 11.
24 Heraclitus *DK* 22 B 42.
25 Testimonia in *DK* 8 A 1–4; see G. Lanata, *Poetica pre-Platonica* (Florence 1963) 104ff.
26 The so-called Derveni papyrus; text in *Zeitschrift für Papyrologie und Epigraphik* 47 (1982) after p. 300.
27 Isocrates 12.236:

> You do not appear to me to have summoned our circle and praised our city without ulterior purpose ('not on one level'), and not as you said to us, but with the intention of testing whether we are concerned with our education ('whether we philosophise') and remember what has been said in our discussions, and whether we are capable of recognising the manner in which the speech has been composed. (δοκεῖς δέ μοι ποιήσασθαι τήν τε παράκλησιν τὴν ἡμετέραν καὶ τὸν ἔπαινον τὸν τῆς πόλεως οὐχ ἁπλῶς, οὐδ᾽ ὡς διείλεξαι πρὸς ἡμᾶς, ἀλλ᾽ ἡμῶν μὲν πεῖραν λαβεῖν βουλόμενος, εἰ φιλοσοφοῦμεν καὶ μεμνήμεθα Τῶυ ἐν ταῖς διατριβαῖς λεγομένων καὶ συνιδεῖν δυνηθεῖμεν ἂν ὃν τρόπον ὁ λόγος τυγχάνει γεγραμμένος.)

See further *PSP* 360 with n. 42; M. Erler, 'Hilfe und Hintersinn. Isokrates' Panathenaikos und die Schriftkritik im Phaidros', in L. Rossetti (ed.), *Proceedings of the II Symposium Platonicum* (St. Augustin 1992) 122–137.
28 Isocrates 12.265:

> I said nothing in response to his further allegations – neither that he had hit on my intention with its covert meanings, nor that he had missed it, but left him in the position in which he had brought himself. (περὶ δὲ τῶν ἄλλων οὐδὲν ἐφθεγξάμην ὧν εἶπεν, οὔθ᾽ ὡς ἔτυχεν ταῖς ὑπονοίαις τῆς

121

NOTES

ἐμῆς διανοίας, οὔθ' ὡς διήμαρτεν, ἀλλ' εἴων αὐτὸν οὕτως ἔχειν ὥσπερ αὐτὸς αὐτὸν διέθηκεν).

29 *Republic* 1, 332b9 ἠνίξατο ἄρα . . . ὁ Σιμωνίδης.
30 See Karl Albert, *Über Platons Begriff der Philosophie* (St Augustin 1989). Albert develops Plato's concept of philosophy primarily from the evidence of the *Symposium* and the *Phaedrus*, without addressing the earlier advance interpretation in the *Protagoras*. See also p. 116f.
31 *Protagoras* 347e3–7: οὕς [sc. τοὺς ποιητάς] οὔτε ἀνερέσθαι οἷόν τ' ἐστὶν περὶ ὧν λέγουσιν, ἐπαγόμενοί τε αὐτοὺς οἱ πολλοὶ ἐν τοῖς λόγοις οἱ μὲν ταῦτά φασιν τὸν ποιητὴν νοεῖν, οἱ δ' ἕτερα, περὶ πράγματος διαλεγόμενοι ὃ ἀδυνατοῦσι ἐξελέγξαι.
32 *Phaedrus* 276e5 διαλεκτικὴ τέχνη; cf. 266c1 διαλεκτικός.
33 See *Phaedrus* 274a and 246a – two typical 'gaps'.
34 Gerhard J. Baudy, *Adonisgärten. Studien zur antiken Samensymbolik* (Frankfurt a.M. 1986).
35 Cf. ἔγκαρπα 276b2, ἄκαρποι 277a1; ἔχοντες σπέρμα 277a1, σπέρματα 276b2, c5.
36 Cf. e.g. *Republic* 534a7 πολλαπλασίων λόγων, 504b2 μακροτέρα περίοδος, 435d3 μακροτέρα ὁδός; *Phaedrus* 274a2 μακρὰ περίοδος, 246a μακρὰ διήγησις; *Parmenides* 136d1–137a6, esp. a5 τοσούτων πέλαγος λόγων.
37 In introducing possibilities which will be realised in the future, Plato can refer to himself without making 'Socrates' commit an anachronism. Scholars have been right to relate the 'great man' of the future in *Charmides* 169a in this sense to Plato. Here in the *Phaedrus* he could just as easily have outlined a 'future' use of writing in accordance with the modern theory of the dialogues. But this was precisely what he did not intend to do.
38 See p. 92 on the theme of 'opening' in the Socratic dialogues.
39 See above, n. 14.
40 διαιρέσεις and ὅροι. The attempt has even been made to relate the *aides-mémoire* (ὑπομνήματα) to the theory of recollection, or anamnesis (C.L. Griswold, *Self-Knowledge in Plato's Phaedrus* (New Haven and London 1986)). If what is meant by this is the capacity of the signs of writing to induce the soul directly to recollect the Ideas which have been seen in the other world, such an interpretation would of course scarcely fit the intention of the critique of writing.
41 276e1–3: 'It is a wonderful game, Socrates, which you are opposing to an insignificant one: the game of a person who knows how to play with speeches by telling stories about justice and the other matters you have mentioned.' Since the *Republic* in fact describes itself as a μυθολογεῖν (*mythologein*; 376d, 501e), there can be no doubt that Plato is referring to his major work (so already W. Luther, 'Die Schwäche des geschriebenen Logos', *Gymnasium* 68 (1961) 536f.).
42 A passage in Aristotle seems relevant here. The aim of ethics is happiness; but this must be something lasting, and thus must be based upon the most lasting human qualities and abilities, i.e. the possession of virtues and knowledge (*EN* 1100a32–b22). If one wanted to make happiness dependent on the vicissitudes of fate one would make the

happy man (the εὐδαίμων) 'into a kind of chameleon' (1100b6). In Plato, however, the figure who corresponds with the Aristotelian εὐδαίμων and his θεωρία is the φιλόσοφος, for whom the διαλεκτικὴ τέχνη creates the εὐδαιμονία which is possible for humans (*Phaedrus* 276e5–277a4): he is no chameleon either.

43 *Phaedrus* 235b, 236b: ἄλλα πλείω καὶ πλείονος ἄξια, which is clearly a synonym for *timiôtera*. For an interpretation of this passage see *PSP* 28–30.

44 Of course that does not mean that Isocrates is thereby declared to be a philosopher in the Platonic sense: μείζω is a comparative expression, like *timiôtera* and πλείονος ἄξια: what Isocrates did at the end of his career was indeed 'more important' than what he had begun with, but it was still far removed from the *timiôtera* of the Platonic philosopher.

45 *Republic* 509a4–5 μειζόνως τιμητέον τὴν τοῦ ἀγαθοῦ ἕξιν, 509b9–10 πρεσβείᾳ καὶ δυνάμει ὑπερέχοντος [sc. τοῦ ἀγαθοῦ] (πρεσβείᾳ means nothing other than τιμῇ).

46 *Republic* 508e2–509a4.

47 See for example Aristotle, *EN* 1101b11, 1102a4, a20, 1141a20, b3, 1178a1; *Metaphysics* 1026a21, 1074b21; *De Partibus Animalium* 644b25; Theophrastus, *Metaphysics* 6b28, 7b14, 10b26, 11a23 (on Speusippus).

48 Similarly *Metaphysics* 983a5–7, 1026a21; *De Partibus Animalium* 644b32.

49 On the outline of situations involving 'support' in sections (a) and (b) see further the detailed interpretations of the relevant dialogues in *PSP*.

50 *Republic* 2, 362d9, 368b4, b7, c1, c5.

51 See 445c5 ἐπειδὴ ἐνταῦθα ἀναβεβήκαμεν τοῦ λόγου.

52 *Laws* 10, 891a5–7 ~ *Republic* 2, 368b7–c1:

'It appears to me even to be impious ("not pious") not to support these logoi' ~ 'I fear it might even be impious ("not pious") to stand by whenever justice is scorned and to be found wanting and not to support it' (οὐδὲ ὅσιον ἔμοιγε εἶναι φαίνεται τὸ μὴ οὐ βοηθεῖν τούτοις τοῖς λόγοις ~ δέδοικα γὰρ μὴ οὐδ᾽ ὅσιον ᾖ παραγενόμενον δικαιοσύνῃ κακηγορουμένῃ ἀπαγορεύειν καὶ μὴ βοηθεῖν).

53 Just as in the lead-in to the 'support' in the second book of the *Republic* (see above, n. 50), expressions denoting support are found in abundance: 890d4 ἐπίκουρον γίγνεσθαι (cf. *Republic* 368c3 ἐπικουρεῖν), 891a5–7 (text above, n. 52), 891b3–4 ἐπαμύνοντες λόγοι, b4–6 νόμοις βοηθεῖν.

54 See *Charmides* 163d, *Menon* 87b–c, *Republic* 533e, *Politicus* 261e.

55 Likewise Protagoras, whom we regard as an important thinker, is not a *philosophos* according to Platonic thinking, which is the reason why the overall thrust of the dialogue gives a negative answer to the decisive question put to him whether he will be capable of supporting his logos (εἰ οἷός τ᾽ ἔσῃ τῷ σαυτοῦ λόγῳ βοηθεῖν, *Protagoras* 341d8).

56 In my 'Sokrates' Spott über Geheimhaltung. Zum Bild des φιλόσοφος in Platons *Euthydemus*', I have tried to give an explanation for the

numerous and remarkably close contacts between the *Euthydemus'* caricature of the philosopher and the picture of the philosopher in the
critique of writing. Holding back knowledge, which Socrates ironically
ascribes to Euthydemus, is something which he practises himself, as is
shown by allusions to the doctrine of anamnesis and the concept of
dialectic. See pp. 76–78 and 86.

57 In this context we must naturally also recall the mythical picture of
the ascent of the 'chariot of souls' to the 'place beyond the heavens'
(*Phaedrus* 246aff.), even if, among the objects for contemplation in the
world beyond (247d–e), no one principle is specified there as the prime
principle of the others.

58 René Schaerer (*La question platonicienne* (Paris and Neuchâtel, 1938,
1969²) and Paul Friedländer (*Platon*, 1928, 1975³) are among the
scholars whose opinions have been most influential.

59 One need only think of the 'place beyond the heavens' as the locality of
the Ideas (*Phaedrus* 247cff.), or even of the 'approximation to God',
which in its very nature is an approximation to the orderliness of the
world of the Ideas (*Republic* 500b–d).

60 On the difference beween 'esotericism' on the one side and 'secret
doctrine' on the other see chapter 26.

61 So Gregory Vlastos in *Gnomon* 35 (1963) 653f.

62 Demonstrating this was the aim of the arguments of Harold Cherniss,
Aristotle's Criticism of Plato and the Academy (Baltimore 1944, 1946²).
The great Aristotelian W.D. Ross, in *Plato's Theory of Ideas* (Oxford
1951) 143, made the following judgment on Cherniss's attempt:

> Aristotle was not the pure blunderer that Prof. Cherniss makes
> him out to have been . . . I do not think for a moment that he
> [sc. Cherniss] has established his case that all that Aristotle says
> about Plato that cannot be verified from the dialogues is pure
> misunderstanding or misrepresentation.

63 See my article 'Die Lückenhaftigkeit der akademischen
Prinzipientheorien nach Aristoteles' Darstellung in Metaphysik M und
N', in A. Graeser (ed.), *Mathematics and Metaphysics in Aristotle. Mathema-
tik und Metaphysik bei Aristoteles* (Bern and Stuttgart 1987) 45–67.

64 On the idea of ascent and the concept of a decisive knowledge of the
Good and the Bad see *PSP* 127–150, esp. 145–148; on the idea of the
archê in the *Lysis*, *PSP* 122f.; see further G. Reale, *Per una nuova interpretazione di Platone*¹⁰ (Milan 1991) 456–459.

65 See *PSP* 141–148.

66 Of special importance among the numerous passages in Aristotle which
attest to the ontological priority of numbers over geometric shapes is
Fragment 2 Ross, from the Περὶ τἀγαθοῦ, which is preserved by
Alexander of Aphrodisias in his commentary on the *Metaphysics* (55.20–
26 Hayduck). See also Konrad Gaiser, *Platons ungeschriebene Lehre*²
(Stuttgart 1968) 148 with 372 n. 125.

67 See above, n. 66. Indeed, *Laws* 894a also seems to refer to the same
theory, but this passage itself needs explanation from the indirect
tradition. See also p. 80f.

68 Hans-Georg Gadamer, *Die Idee des Guten zwischen Plato und Aristoteles, Sitzungsberichte der Heidelberger Akademie der Wissenschaften, Philos.-histor. Klasse* 1978, 3 (Heidelberg 1978) 82.
69 For a discussion of the limitations of the discourse in the *Gorgias* see *PSP* 191–207, esp, 199–204.
70 Aristotle, *Metaphysics* A6, 987b14–18 and Z1, 1028b19, according to which Plato gave the objects of mathematics an ontological middle position (see also W. D. Ross, *Aristotle's Metaphysics* (Oxford 1924) I, 166).
71 On the problem of *psychê* and *mathêmatika* in Plato see Philip Merlan, *From Platonism to Neoplatonism*³ (The Hague 1968) 13ff., 45ff.; Gaiser, *Platons ungeschriebene Lehre*² 44ff., 89ff.
72 Hermann Keulen, *Untersuchungen zu Platons 'Euthydem'* (Wiesbaden 1971) 25–40 and 49–56; see also Paul Friedländer, *Platon* II³ (Berlin 1964) 171, 177f.
73 On the other hand, writing necessarily involves the separation of production and use: author and reader generally do not even know one another. This 'alienation', which is inherent in its nature, makes writing basically incapable of fulfilling the requirements of true 'rhetoric' (λόγων τέχνη).
74 See pp. 28–35, 74f.
75 'Die Schwäche des geschriebenen Logos' 536f.
76 Gaiser, *Platons ungeschriebene Lehre*² 187.
77 Ibid. 173–189, esp. 175 and 187–189; see also Gaiser, *Platone come scrittore filosofico* (Naples 1984) 148f.
78 On the problems of the passage and its discussion in the literature on Plato, see my article 'Unsterblichkeit und Trichotomie der Seele im zehnten Buch der Politeia', *Phronesis* 21 (1976) 31–58.
79 On 'opening' the dialogues (*Symposium* 221d–222a) see p. 92f.
80 Heraclitus *DK* 22 B 93.
81 On Alcibiades see further p. 91f.
82 Friedrich Schleiermacher, Introduction to the translation of Plato, vol. I.1 (Berlin 1804) 15.
83 Ibid., Introduction to the *Phaedrus*, 52.
84 For a detailed criticism of the methodological deficiencies and factual errors of Schleiermacher and his followers see *PSP* 331–375 (Appendix 1: Die moderne Theorie der Dialogform).
85 One of my aims in *PSP* was to demonstrate the congruity between Plato's theory of the use of writing and the literary shaping of the dialogues. On the observations in pp. 85–93 see the more detailed analyses to be found there.
86 See pp. 76–78.
87 See pp. 15f. and 63f.
88 See the brief discussion on p. 16 as well as the chapter on the *Republic* in *PSP* 271–326.
89 See p. 77f.
90 See p. 70 and *PSP* 307f. with n. 99.
91 Of course, it is not my object to attempt a comprehensive stock-taking (let alone a final balance-sheet) of Platonic irony here.
92 This is accepted even among commentators of an unambiguously

'antimetaphysical' orientation; see e.g. G. Vlastos, *Platonic Studies* (Princeton 1973) 397: 'Could anyone say that Plato felt anything less than veneration for the Ideas?'

93 See *PSP* 87f.; likewise, I have demonstrated that interpretations which deal solely with the aspect of irony are inadequate for the other early works as well. See now also Erler, *Der Sinn der Aporien in den Dialogen Platons*.

94 *Phaedrus* 246a. On the passage see p. 67f.

95 At *Politicus* 304c10–d2 there is a discussion of a type of oratory which convinces the many 'with knowledge' (i.e. *lege artis*) 'by means of story-telling, but not by instructing' (διὰ μυθολογίας ἀλλὰ μὴ διὰ διδαχῆς). It might be deduced from this that for Plato influencing people verbally without instruction (i.e. by means of *personal* instruction: writing stays ἄνευ διδαχῆς, *Phaedrus* 275a7) falls under the category of *mythologia*. Meanwhile, it remains questionable whether the passage can be applied to the dialogues: for they indeed reach the many (no author can avoid that), but do not aim to convince the many *qua* multitude (πλῆθος).

96 The fact that Plato is aware that one and the same text will be interpreted differently by different listeners or readers naturally does not mean that he lived in the belief that he was in possession of a literary technique which could reliably direct such different responses. On these matters see Chapters 9–11 and 19.

97 In a very balanced discussion, Gaiser, *Platone come scrittore filosofico* 125–152, esp. 134–136, argued in favour of myth's equivalence to logos. The approach which subordinates myth to logos has been represented by among others G. Müller, 'Die Mythen der platonischen Dialoge', *Nachrichten der Gießener Hochschulgesellschaft* 32 (1963) 77–92 (also in *id.*, *Platonische Studien* (Heidelberg 1986) 110–125). The discussion of the theme by G. Cerri, *Platone sociologico della communicazione* (Milan 1991) (17–74 Mito e poesia) is full of excellent observations.

98 To be sure, it can happen that a point of view is represented by two *names*: in the *Republic* Glaucon and Adeimantus together demand a defence of justice by Socrates; Simmias and Cebes together appear in the *Phaedo* as people who doubt the immortality of the soul; Clinias and Megillus together represent Doric culture, the political orderliness of which (εὐνομία) the Athenian in the *Laws* wishes to imitate and surpass. But such twin-figures do not form two independent points of view, and the arguments of the dialectician are mostly directed at any one time only towards one of them, rarely to both at the same time. (Only Clinias and Megillus, who resemble each other almost like twins, are frequently addressed simultaneously.)

99 See p. 87.

100 *Meno* 86d–e (see *PSP* 185f.), likewise *Euthydemus* 287d6 (both times ἄρχειν means 'to command'); see also *Protagoras* 351e8–11, 353b4 (ἡγεμονεῖν means 'to exercise command').

101 In the *Parmenides* the *young* Socrates meets the *old* Eleatic: the striking emphasis on the difference of ages (*Parmenides* 127b–c) obliges us to see even in this conversation a conversation between unequals.

102 Of course there remains the basic dialogical nature of thought as a conversation of the soul with itself; see pp. 20f. and 100f.
103 It should be noted in passing that the aporetic dialogues do not simply revel in ambivalences but can be very unambiguous in their denial of whatever is wrong and mistaken.
104 See G.W.F. Hegel, *Vorlesungen über die Geschichte der Philosophie* (Theorie-Werkausgabe ((Frankfurt a.M. 1971)) vol.19, p. 22): 'from his [sc. Plato's] dialogues his philosophy emerges with absolute clarity. . . . The difference of opinions which emerges is examined; a result arises as the truth.'
105 Literary scholars have been justified in describing a series of authors in concepts which modern interpreters of Plato would like to reserve for the Platonic dialogues. I have collected some references at *PSP* 359 n. 40 (with supplementary material in *Platone e la scrittura della filosofia*[3] (Milan 1992) 448 n. 40).
106 Theognis 681–682; Pindar, *Olympian Odes* 2.83–86. On them see Gregory Nagy, 'Homerische Epik und Pindars Preislieder. Mündlichkeit und Aktualitätsbezug', in Wolfgang Raible (ed.), *Zwischen Festtag und Alltag. Zehn Beiträge zum Thema 'Mündlichkeit und Schriftlichkeit'* (Tübingen 1988) 51–64, esp. 52–53.
107 Aristotle fr. 192 Rose; Aristoxenus fr. 43 Wehrli.
108 Hippasus *DK* 18.4.
109 Iamblichus, *De Vita Pythagorica* 257 (= *DK* 18.5).
110 Hans Joachim Krämer, *Platone e i fondamenti della metafisica* (Milan 1982, 1989[3]); *id.*, 'Fichte, Schlegel und der Infinitismus in der Platon-deutung', *Deutsche Vierteljahrsschrift für Literaturwissenschaft und Geistesgeschichte* 62 (1988) 583–621; Albert, *Über Platons Begriff der Philosophie.*
111 On this point see Albert, *Über Platons Begriff der Philosophie* 20–30, esp. 27.

BIBLIOGRAPHY

Albert, Karl, *Über Platons Begriff der Philosophie, Beiträge zur Philosophie* 1 (St Augustin 1989)

Baudy, Gerhard J., *Adonisgärten. Studien zur antiken Samensymbolik, Beiträge zur klassischen Philologie* 176 (Frankfurt a.M. 1986)

Cerri, Giovanni, *Platone sociologico della communicazione* (Milan 1991)

Cherniss, Harold, *Aristotle's Criticism of Plato and the Academy* (Baltimore 1944, 1946²)

'"Derveni-Papyrus": Der orphische Papyrus von Derveni', *Zeitschrift für Papyrologie und Epigraphik* 47 (1982), printed after p. 300

Diels, Hermann and Kranz, Walther, *Die Fragmente der Vorsokratiker*, 3 vols (I & II Berlin 1951⁶, repr. 1992; III Berlin 1952⁶, repr. 1990)

Edelstein, Ludwig, 'Platonic Anonymity', *American Journal of Philology* 83 (1962) 1–22

Erler, Michael, 'Hilfe und Hintersinn. Isokrates' Panathenaikos und die Schriftkritik im Phaidros', in Livio Rosetti (ed.), *Understanding the Phaedrus. Proceedings of the II Symposium Platonicum, International Plato Studies* 1 (St Augustin 1992)

—— *Der Sinn der Aporien in den Dialogen Platons. Übungsstücke zur Anleitung im philosophischen Denken, Untersuchungen zur antiken Literatur und Geschichte* 25 (Berlin and New York 1987)

Friedländer, Paul, *Platon*, 3 vols (Berlin 1928; I & II 1964³; III Berlin 1975³)

Gadamer, Hans-Georg, *Die Idee des Guten zwischen Plato und Aristoteles, Sitzungsberichte der Heidelberger Akademie der Wissenschaften, Philos.-histor. Klasse* 1978, 3 (Heidelberg 1978)

—— *Platos dialektische Ethik. Phänomenologische Interpretationen zum Philebos* (Leipzig 1931)

—— *Wahrheit und Methode. Grundzüge einer philosophischen Hermeneutik* (Tübingen 1960, 1965²)

Gaiser, Konrad, *Platone come scrittore filosofico. Saggi sull'ermeneutica dei dialoghi platonici, Istituto Italiano per gli Studi Filosofici. Lezione della Scuola di Studi Superiori in Napoli* 2 (Naples 1984)

—— *Platons ungeschriebene Lehre. Studien zur systematischen und geschichtlichen Begründung der Wissenschaften in der Platonischen Schule* (Stuttgart 1963, 1968²)

Griswold, Charles L. Jr., *Self-Knowledge in Plato's Phaedrus* (New Haven and London 1986)

Hegel, Georg Wilhelm Friedrich, *Werke* (Theorie-Werkausgabe), 21 vols (Frankfurt a.M. 1970ff.), vol. 19, *Vorlesungen über die Geschichte der Philosophie 2* (Frankfurt a.M. 1971)

Keulen, Hermann, *Untersuchungen zu Platons 'Euthydem'*, Klassisch-Philologische Studien 37 (Wiesbaden 1971)

Krämer, Hans Joachim, *Arete bei Platon und Aristoteles. Zum Wesen und zur Geschichte der platonischen Ontologie*, Abhandlungen der Heidelberger Akademie der Wissenschaften, *Philos.-histor. Klasse*, 1959, 6 (Heidelberg 1959, Amsterdam 1967²)

—— 'Fichte, Schlegel und der Infinitismus in der Platondeutung', *Deutsche Vierteljahrsschrift für Literaturwissenschaft und Geistesgeschichte* 62 (1988) 583–621

—— *Platone e i fondamenti della metafisica. Saggio sulla teoria dei principi e sulle dottrine non scritte di Platone con una raccolta dei documenti fondamentali in edizione biligue e bibliografia*, tr. Giovanni Reale, *Pubblicazioni del Centro di Ricerche di Metafisica. Sezione di metafisica del Platonismo nel suo sviluppo storico e nella filosofia patristica*, Studi e testi 1 (Milan 1982, 1989³)

Lanata, Giuliana, *Poetica pre-Platonica. Testimonianze e frammenti*, Biblioteca di Studi Superiori. *Filosofia Antica* 43 (Florence 1963)

Luther, Wilhelm, 'Die Schwäche des geschriebenen Logos. Ein Beispiel humanistischer Interpretation, versucht am sogenannten Schriftmythos in Platons Phaidros (274b6ff.)', *Gymnasium* 68 (1961) 526–548

Merkelbach, Reinhold, *Platons Menon* (Frankfurt a.M. 1988)

Merlan, Philip, *From Platonism to Neoplatonism* (The Hague 1953, 1968³)

Merton, Robert King, *The Sociology of Science. Theoretical and Empirical Investigations* (Chicago and London 1973)

Müller, Gerhard, 'Die Mythen der platonischen Dialoge', *Nachrichten der Gießener Hochschulgesellschaft* 32 (1963) 77–92 (repr. in Gerhard Müller, Andreas Graeser and Dieter Maue (eds), *Platonische Studien*, Bibliothek der Altertumswissenschaften N. F. 2. Reihe 76 (Heidelberg 1986), 110–125)

Nagy, Gregory, 'Homerische Epik und Pindars Preislieder. Mündlichkeit und Aktualitätsbezug', in Wolfgang Raible (ed.), *Zwischen Festtag und Alltag. Zehn Beiträge zum Thema 'Mündlichkeit und Schriftlichkeit'*, Script-Oralia 6 (Tübingen 1988) 51–64

Reale, Giovanni, *Per una nuova interpretazione di Platone. Rilettura della metafisica dei grandi dialoghi alla luce delle 'Dottrine non scritte'*, Pubblicazioni del Centro di Ricerche di Metafisica. *Sezione di metafisica del Platonismo nel suo sviluppo storico e nella filosofia patristica*. Studi e testi 3 (Milan 1991¹⁰)

Robin, Léon, *La théorie platonicienne des idées et des nombres d'après Aristote. Étude historique et critique* (Paris 1908, repr. Hildesheim 1963)

Rose, Valentin, *Aristotelis qui ferebantur librorum fragmenta* (Stuttgart 1886, repr. 1967)

Ross, William David, *Aristotelis fragmenta selecta* (Oxford 1955, repr. 1970)

—— *Aristotle's Metaphysics*, 2 vols (Oxford 1924)

—— *Plato's Theory of Ideas* (Oxford 1951, repr. 1976)

Schaerer, René, *La question platonicienne. Étude sur les rapports de la pensée et de l'expression dans les dialogues*, Mémoires d'Université de Neuchâtel 10 (Paris and Neuchâtel 1938, 1969²)

Schleiermacher, Friedrich, *Platons Werke* (Berlin 1804ff., 1817ff.²; vol. I.1, 1804, 1817²)

Stein, Heinrich von, *Sieben Bücher zur Geschichte des Platonismus. Untersuchungen über das System des Plato und sein Verhältnis zur späteren Theologie und Philosophie*, 3 parts (Göttingen 1862/1864/1875, repr. Frankfurt a.M. 1965)

Szlezák, Thomas Alexander, 'Die Lückenhaftigkeit der akademischen Prinzipientheorien nach Aristoteles' Darstellung in Metaphysik M und N', in Andreas Graeser (ed.), *Mathematics and Metaphysics in Aristotle. Mathematik und Metaphysik bei Aristoteles. Akten des X. Symposium Aristotelicum Sigriswil, 6–12. September 1984, Berner Reihe philosophischer Studien 6* (Bern and Stuttgart 1987) 45–67

—— *Platon und die Schriftlichkeit der Philosophie. Interpretationen zu den frühen und mittleren Dialogen* (Berlin and New York 1985) (= *PSP*) (supplementary material in *Platone e la scrittura della filosofia* (Milan 1992³))

—— 'Sokrates' Spott über Geheimhaltung. Zum Bild des φιλόσοφος in Platons *Euthydemus*', *Antike und Abendland* 26 (1980) 75–89

—— 'Unsterblichkeit und Trichotomie der Seele im zehnten Buch der Politeia', *Phronesis* 21 (1976) 31–58

Tennemann, Wilhelm Gottlieb, *System der Platonischen Philosophie*, 4 vols (Leipzig 1792–1795)

Vlastos, Gregory, Review of Krämer, *Arete bei Platon und Aristoteles* (1959), *Gnomon* 35 (1963) 641–655

—— *Platonic Studies* (Princeton 1973)

Wehrli, Fritz, *Die Schule des Aristoteles. Text und Kommentar*, 10 vols (Basel 1944ff., repr. Basel and Stuttgart 1967/1968; 2 suppl. vols 1974 and 1978); 2: *Aristoxenos* (1945, 1967²)

Wilpert, Paul, *Zwei aristotelische Frühschriften über die Ideenlehre* (Regensburg 1949)

Wittgenstein, Ludwig, *Vermischte Bemerkungen. Eine Auswahl aus dem Nachlaß*, edited by Georg Henrik von Wright with the collaboration of Heikki Nyman, *Bibliothek Suhrkamp* 535 (Frankfurt a.M. 1977)

INDEX OF PASSAGES CITED

INDEX OF PASSAGES CITED

BIOGRAPHICAL NOTE

Thomas Alexander Szlezák, born in 1940, studied Classics, Philosophy and History from 1959 to 1967 at the universities of Erlangen, Munich and Tübingen. He gained his doctorate at the Technische Universität in Berlin in 1969, with a thesis dealing with late-antique interpretations of Aristotle (*Pseudo-Archytas über die Kategorien. Texte zur griechischen Aristoteles-Exegese*, publ. 1972). He obtained his post-doctoral lecturing qualification in 1976 at Zurich University with a thesis entitled *Platon und Aristoteles in der Nuslehre Plotins* (publ. 1979), in which Plotinus' methods of the philosophical interpretation of the 'Classics', Plato and Aristotle were for the first time subjected to systematic philosophical analysis. There followed several years of research and teaching as a private lecturer in Zurich, from where, in 1983, he moved to the Chair of Classics at Würzburg University. *Platon und die Schriftlichkeit der Philosophie* appeared in 1985. The interpretations offered there of the early and middle dialogues of Plato demonstrate that the prevalent view of the dialogues as self-sufficient works (which thus do not need any supplementation by means of Plato's oral philosophy) is contradicted by Plato's text itself – a conclusion which has radically altered the controversy over the last decades about Plato's unwritten philosophy of principles. The book has also appeared in Italian (Milan 1989, 1992³). The first edition of the present volume was also published in Italy (Milan 1991, 1992²). Translations into other languages followed (French 1996, Spanish 1997, Polish 1998, Swedish 1999). Szlezák's other main research areas include fifth-century Greek tragedy as well as Aristotle's *Metaphysics*; a series of essays and reviews on these fields has appeared in recent years. Szlezák has been teaching at the University of Tübingen since 1990.